The
Carob Way
to Health

The
Carob Way
to Health

*All-Natural Recipes
for Cooking with
Nature's Healthful
Chocolate Alternative*

Frances Sheridan
Goulart

WARNER BOOKS
A Warner Communications Company

Warner Books, Inc., 75 Rockefeller Plaza, New York, N.Y. 10019

A Warner Communications Company

Printed in the United States of America

First printing: November 1982
10 9 8 7 6 5 4 3 2 1

Designed by Richard Oriolo

Library of Congress Cataloging in Publication Data

Goulart, Frances Sheridan.
  The carob way to health.

  1. Cookery (Carob) I. Title.
TX814.5.C35G68   641.6'446   82-7104
ISBN 0-446-37302-8 (U.S.A.)   AACR2
ISBN 0-446-37315-X (Canada)

To Day
who showed me how to do it.

To Susan Asanovic
who showed me how to do it
a little bit better.

And to
Esme Carroll
as always.

Contents

The Carob Way to Health

1
Carob in Health

The American people are full of beans—mostly cocoa beans. The United States Census Bureau says that each year we go through 850,000 tons of cocoa beans in the form of chocolate candies, cakes, cookies, ice cream, beverages, and other chocolate confections. And all of it is rich in saturated fats, sugar, caffeine, chemicals, and empty calories.

The carob is a fleshy pod that grows in the Middle East. It has been used for food for many centuries, and when properly prepared has a flavor similar to chocolate. (The history and lore of this fascinating food will be more fully explored in Chapter 2.)

Nutritionally, carob is everything that chocolate is not. Gram for gram, carob contains three times the calcium that milk does. It is high in phosphorus and potassium, plus it contains some sodium and iron. Furthermore, carob is 7 percent crude fat (cocoa has 23 percent) and has 40 percent fewer calories than cocoa and 65 percent fewer calories than an equal amount of sweet chocolate. Also, carob contains no caffeine or other stimulants. As an added bonus, it has 46 percent natural sugar, where cocoa has only 5½ percent.

This is what Jeffrey Blish, author of *The Dictionary of Health Foods** has to say about chocolate:

> Chocolate is very high in calories, fats, and carbohydrates. It may also irritate skin problems, especially adolescent acne, and in many persons cause an allergic reaction. Chocolate has a tendency to cause constipation, and it should be avoided by those with decay, because it has a tendency to find its way into the nooks and crannies of the teeth and feed the decay bacteria there. Chocolate is also high in cholesterol and saturated fats, since one of its main components is cocoa butter, so it should be avoided by those concerned about their cholesterol level... [yet] chocolate is one of America's best-loved flavorings...

With friends like this who needs enemies?

Some of chocolate's troublemaking ingredients are put there, some occur naturally.

Experiments have shown, for instance, says one research study reported in the *Food and Cosmetic Toxicology* journal, that tannins, which produce chocolate's excessive astringency in the mouth, and which are richly supplied by chocolate, may be considerably more dangerous than previously imagined. Tannin-containing foods, such as chocolate, can depress the growth of young animals, studies suggest, since they bind with protein to form indigestible compounds, reducing the absorption of protein through the intestinal wall. And, says researcher Carol S. Farkas (of the University of Waterloo in Ontario, Canada), "Tan-

*Published by Nash Publishing in 1972.

nin combines with iron and inhibits its absorption by the body."

At least one medical journal (*Minnesota Medicine 1976 Annual*) has warned that another natural constituent of chocolate, phenylethylamine, is suspected as a cause of migraine headaches.

Untold thousands who suffer from headaches and visual disturbance as an allergic reaction to chocolate are unaware of the cause, since their distress may occur as much as six to ten hours *after* ingesting the chocolate bar, brownie, or hot fudge sundae.

But that's not all. According to Ohio cancer surgeon John P. Minton, "Chocolate (also tea and cola) apparently contains a nitrogen compound known as methylxanthine which triggers cell growth by extending the activity of a certain cell chemical. Of the 47 women who participated in the study, 67 percent experienced disappearance of their cysts after eliminating chocolate, tea, and colas."*

Furthermore, for the millions of food-allergy sufferers, chocolate ranks with eggs, wheat, and milk as a major offender. According to allergist Dr. John Baron, the culprit may well be coal-tar sensitivity. "This is one of the problems caused by artificial flavorings and colorings found in... all chocolate," he says.**

Chocolate, or theobromine cocoa, was once called the food of the gods, but it's hardly fit for human consumption any more. There's no such thing as fresh chocolate or pure chocolate. According to chocolate authority L. Russell Cook, beans intended for a "blend" are cleaned, crushed, roasted, fermented, dutched (treated with an alkalizer to neutralize acids

---

*East-West Journal (December 1979).
**Bestways (September 1979).

and darken color), or conched (cooked to develop a nut-like flavor). All this even before being heated and honed into the final product.

Not only does a hot cup of chocolate provide only "mousey" amounts of important vitamins and minerals, it may even provide a few rat hairs as well. According to the FDA's "Filth Guidelines in Food," ground cocoa beans are permitted to contain an "average of 75 microscopic insect fragments per 50 gm., when six 50-gm. subsamples are examined...and an average of 2 rodent hairs per 50 gm. when six 50-gm. subsamples are examined; or if any one subsample contains 5 rodent hairs."*

And, because of its high-fat content, chocolate can and often does act as a carrier of a salmonella bacteria, a type of food poisoning characterized by nausea, vomiting, and diarrhea. Sometimes brand-name chocolate candy bars come contaminated with carcinogenic weed killers and wood preservatives, such as lindane, BHC, or eplaclor eposide. Traces of these and other dangerous substances were found by the independent testing laboratories of WARF Institute in 1976 in five brands of top-selling candy bars (although the EPA safety levels supposedly do not permit any of these to be present).

Dr. Samuel Epstein, professor of occupational and environmental medicine at the University of Illinois School of Public Health, adds that, "The substances are all cancer-causing agents, and when kids eat substantial amounts of candy, these chemicals can accumulate in the body's fatty tissues."

---

*From *Eating May Be Hazardous to Your Health*, by Jacqueline Verrett and Jean Carper (Anchor Books, 1975).

Even in its *un*contaminated state, chocolate has a tendency to provoke "rectal itch" and allergic responses in large numbers of children and adults, and to irritate such skin conditions as adolescent acne.

The real villain, of course, is chocolate's high sugar content, which contributes heavily to tooth decay and other physical problems, including obesity. One candy bar may contain as much as 15 teaspoons of sugar. A 3-ounce serving of milk chocolate provides almost 500 calories, while semisweet or dark chocolate actually contains more sugar than milk chocolate to make it more palatable.

While chocolate is a robber of nutrients essential for dental, mental, and whole-body health, carob is a replenisher. Carob is nonaddictive, virtually nonallergic, and a boon for the hyperactive child or adult. Studies indicate that children who are allergic to chocolate can, in most cases, safely consume carob.

Carob is low in fat and particularly rich in calcium (352 mg. per 100 grams, or 1,597 mg. per pound). By comparison, milk, considered an excellent source of calcium, has only 120 to 130 mg. calcium per 100 grams, or 530 to 550 mg. calcium per pound. Furthermore, carob contains none of the harmful caffeine or oxalic acid (as chocolate does) that interferes with the body's ability to assimilate calcium.

Carob is rich in protein and high in natural carbohydrates. Although very sweet, it is 60 percent lower in calories than chocolate and readily assimilated. Carob also has twice the bowel-regulating fiber of chocolate (see page 148) and is a good source of pectin.

And, as for vitamins, consider this: Carob has as much thiamine (B_1) as asparagus or strawberries, as much niacin (B_3) as lima beans, lentils, or peas, and more vitamin A than eggplant, asparagus, and beets.

So, why settle for the touch-and-go power of chocolate?

2
Carob in History

In 1979, Americans bought 2.9 billion pounds of candy, 55 percent of it chocolate. In fact, 85 percent of the cocoa consumed in this country is in the form of chocolate candy. Of this chocolate total, 714 million pounds were in the form of candy bars, 684 million pounds were packaged goods (including assorted chocolates), 114 million pounds were specialty candies, such as chocolate eggs, and 86 million pounds were chocolates sold in bulk.*

And the rest of the world isn't far behind. Just compare the figures below:

Country	Metric Tons of Cocoa Beans Used (1978)
USSR	90,000
Netherlands	126,000
Brazil	136,000
United Kingdom	72,000

The bittersweet truth is that we have become a nation of chocoholics—overweight and undernourished.

Has this been the way of the world from the

---

*From *The Changing American Diet*, published by the Center for Science in the Public Interest (1978), Washington, D.C.

beginning? Indeed not. At one time we did most of our fudging, man and beast alike, with nature's chocolate alternative, the carob. A member of the legume family, the carob has always been an important farm crop in the Mediterranean basin and other hot and semiarid regions. It was cultivated by the Greeks and carried as far west as Spain and Morocco by the Arabs.

In the Bible, there is the prodigal son who "would fain have filled his belly with the husks that the swine did eat..." (Luke 15:16). Those husks could have been carob pods. And many are convinced that the "locusts" that John the Baptist ate were carob pods. Which is why the carob is still popularly known as St. John's bread and sometimes as locust pod (Matthew 3:4).

But some horticultural historians claim that carob is not a locust at all. According to a Department of Agriculture bulletin, "People started calling the carob a locust because it resembles the various locust trees that adorn our native forests. Both yield tough, durable wood and bear foliage, like clusters or large rose leaves. The carob and all the locusts welcome the spring with dainty sprigs of fragrant blossoms that turn to bean-type pods in the fall. But the carob is an evergreen and the locusts are not. Its blossoms are deep red and locust blossoms range from creamy white to rusty pink. Locust beans come in fragile, greenish yellow pods. The carob bears a large thick pod of chocolate brown..."

The carob is also mentioned in the Talmud. One ancient Hebrew reference work tells about a young rabbi who came upon an old man who was planting a carob seed beside the road. When the rabbi remarked that the man would be long dead when the tree bore fruit, the old man replied, "I plant not for myself but for those who come after me." Then the young rabbi lay down to rest. And, shades of Rip Van Winkle, he awoke seventy years later to find the carob tree full of fruit and himself an old man in unfamiliar surroundings.

In the fourth century B.C., the Greek Theophrastus remarked that some people in his day called the carob the Egyptian fig. And from a temple at Idfu (in Egypt) comes an ancient prescription whose ingredients include essence of the carob bean.

The authors of *Food in Antiquity** tell us that, "The word for sweetness in Egypt is generally associated with the carob or locust bean, but apart from seeds and pods found there in tombs from as early as the Twelfth Dynasty there is little we can learn about its use. It is thought to have grown wild on the coasts of Syria and Anatolia, but there is not much information about its culinary use there, either. According to Pliny, [carob] signifies the sycamore fig, which is far more likely they say, but Columella is the first to talk of growing the carob. It was eaten by the Romans green and fresh, when its taste was sweet; when dried, Pliny says it should be soaked in water for several days before use."

Carob has always been a somewhat quixotic food. According to the *Standard Cyclopedia of Horticulture***:

> The Ceratonia (which is the Greek word for horn) is known also as Algaroba, Karoub, Caroubler, and St. John's Bread. The dry valves or pods have been supposed to be the husks that provided the subsistence of the prodigal son. *The*

---

*Published by Praeger Books, 1969.
**Published by Macmillan Company, New York, in 1950.

seeds are said to have been the original carat weight of goldsmiths.

Food historian I. C. Furnes adds:

Precious jewels and carob beans have been cherished by man for centuries... the word 'carat,' which is used to measure the weight of gem stones, is derived from the Arabic word 'quirat,' which, in turn, comes from the Greek 'keration,' meaning carob beans or small weight.*

The carob not only kept the prodigal son alive but others as well. Wellington's cavalry used it as their main form of sustenance in the Peninsular campaign, as did the British cavalry at Malta, where they called it "honey locust." And, during the Second World War, the people of southern Greece were able to survive the German occupation because they could still pick the carob pods.

Today, in Italy, Greece, Spain, Yugoslavia, and Portugal, the large pods, which are rich in protein (8 percent) and sugar (46 percent), are a very important forage crop for all kinds of livestock. And in times of scarcity, the carob tree has furnished sustenance to the poor in the form of fermented drinks, powders, and flours, says carob historian J. Eliot Coit.**

In North America this beautiful perennial, which has hibiscus-like flowers, can be found in bogs and water meadows from the Canadian Maritime Provinces and Pennsylvania, westward and northward to Wisconsin. In some areas it is also called "Water Avens."

---

*From *Anatomy of Paradise*, 1937.
***Fruit Varieties and Horticultural Digest*, January 1967.

The early settlers here called it Indian chocolate. They used it as a standard home remedy to cure dysentery, diarrhea, and stomach upsets.

The U.S. Patent Office took a hand in promoting the carob tree in this country. In 1854, it imported seedlings from Alicante, Spain. In 1859, it imported more seedlings from Palestine. About 8,000 plants were grown in the state of Washington and distributed in the spring of 1860, mostly to the southern states. Some of these plants did find their way to California, because there are now a number of old trees growing in various parts of the state from San Diego in the south to Napa and Butte counties in the north.

Cultivation and Processing

The carob tree is actually a handsome evergreen with sickle-shaped pods, 4 to 12 inches long, each containing 5 to 15 inedible hard seeds. Siliqua, the only species now widely found in warm climates, is grown for both shade and edible pods. This variety, which grows to a height of 40 to 50 feet, thrives in southern California and southern Florida, wherever a hot climate with an abundance of rain prevails.

While the carob is a rather slow grower, it lives to a great age. Fruit may be expected 5 years from budding. In California, seedlings bear when 6 to 8 years of age and yield between 450 and 700 pounds of pods. At 12 years, the yield may be as much as 5,000 pounds per acre. Many trees are known to last for over 100 years, still bearing fruit.

Better than 1,700,000 pounds of pods a year are harvested in Palestine, Syria, and especially on the island of Cyprus. (The United States uses only 12 to 15 million pounds of this yearly harvest.)

Carob by-products go into everything from ice cream to mustard. Carob is also used to flavor vitamins, tobacco, and dog biscuits and to promote chemical functions in some pharmaceuticals.

The carob seeds, which are inedible unless processed, are widely used in the manufacture of the food additive gum *Tragacanth* (locust bean gum). In ancient Egypt, the gum was used as an adhesive in mummy bindings. Today it serves as a stabilizer in processed foods. It improves the texture and freeze-melt characteristics of ice cream, thickens salad dressings, pie fillings, and barbecue sauces, and makes softer, more resilient cakes and biscuits. Spain, Portugal, Italy, and Greece fill America's demand for this gum.

An oil called algaroba is also extracted from the seeds and used for medical purposes.

Processing the carob pod is a relatively uncomplicated procedure, especially when compared to the manufacture of chocolate. According to Vermont's Springtree Corporation, this country's largest user of carob, the powder is usually produced in the following manner:

> When the ripened, partly-dry pods have been harvested, they are broken up into small pieces called "kibbies." (The seeds are separated and sold for industrial use.) Only about 10 to 15 percent of the Mediterranean area's finest kibbled carob is selected and brought to California where it is specially roasted and finely ground into powder. Various batches of powder are then carefully blended.
>
> Carob in raw or toasted form contains the entire locust fruit except for the seeds which are processed into industrial gums. The fruit flesh is

processed into pulp, dried, toasted, and pulverized into the final product. To maximize the significant amounts of natural sugar and many vitamins, the degree of roast is important. If too dark, carob loses sugar and becomes bitter; important vitamins also disappear. If too light, the dissolution properties of the product are adversely affected. Optimum roast permits enough sweetness, large amounts of nutritious vitamins, and ideal dissolution properties. Equally important is the fitness of the grind. In order to be good, pulverized carob must pass through a 0.05 square millimeter sieve.

How is carob syrup manufactured? The following is a description given by Vermont's Whitney Brook Farm:

> The process used in Crete (where the oldest and tastiest pods are said to grow) to derive powder and syrup from the carob tree is still fairly primitive. Carob pods are collected in the fall from the ground under wild trees (there are no cultivated carob orchards in Crete). The pods are washed and broken to separate the beans from the pod. The broken pods are then cooked to 183 degrees Fahrenheit, until they thicken into pure carob sugar syrup. (The pods actually dissolve like any other fructose when cooked.) The syrup is filtered once to eliminate any pieces that do not dissolve. It is then poured into 55-gallon drums for shipping. Carob syrup can be used with carob powder or alone. It is rich in carob flavor, but short on carob color.

Therefore, Whitney Brook Farm recommends using 80 percent syrup and 20 percent powder in basic baking recipes.

The future for carob looks very bright. With the cost of cocoa beans up over 300 percent over 1975 prices, the moderately priced carob looks very economical, indeed. And, we are all interested in using natural ingredients to replace those artificial flavors and colors we have learned to mistrust.

Growing Your Own Carob

The trees need very little pruning and no spraying because they are remarkably free from fungus diseases and insect pests. In most soils they need no fertilization until they come into bearing.

At maturity, the pods drop to the ground or can be shaken down where they are easily gathered.

Carob can also be grown as a houseplant. The seeds should germinate readily and the plant should be provided with a lot of sunlight in an atmosphere almost similar to that of a greenhouse.

3
Cooking with Carob

Your first experience with carob should probably be with the store-bought product. You can buy carob in block, chip, powder or syrup form at a good health food store or even the nutritional section of some supermarkets. After you've become more familiar with cooking with carob, you might want to roast and grind your own. For more on that see the second half of this chapter.

Using Carob As a Substitute

1. The recipes in this book use *unsweetened* carob powder. You may use roasted (toasted), home-grown, or store-bought carob powder interchangeably.

2. Carob syrup can be homemade or store-bought. Honey may be substituted in most cases.

3. Carob chips or blocks and bars may be used interchangeably where the carob is to be chopped, grated, or melted.

4. To substitute carob powder for cocoa, use the same amount of carob powder *or* ¾ cup carob powder plus ¼ cup dry milk powder.

5. To replace 1 square (1 ounce) of semisweet chocolate, use 3 tablespoons unsweetened carob powder plus 1 tablespoon of water. (You can also add 1 or 2 drops of pure vanilla extract and 1 teaspoon liquid lecithin or granular lecithin for smoothness.)

6. To replace 1 cup unsweetened melted chocolate, use the recipe for Desweetened Carob Syrup on page 32.

7. Finely chopped, naturally dried fruits, such as apricots, figs, and especially dates, may be substituted for carob chips in many recipes unless otherwise specified.

8. Use maple syrup, sorghum, or any natural liquid sweetener—with or without 1 or more tablespoons of carob powder—to replace light or dark corn syrup.

9. To replace 1 cup of molasses (not blackstrap), use either of the following:

- a. ¾ cup natural liquid sweetener plus 2 tablespoons carob powder, *or*
- b. ¼ cup honey plus ¾ cup carob syrup or maple syrup

10. To replace brown sugar, try equal parts of the following:

- a. Carob meal (page 27) plus date sugar, *or*
- b. Any homemade fruit sugar (page 20), plus carob powder, *or*
- c. Oven-dried sprouted wheat kernels, which have been ground to a powder.

Honey and Other Natural Sweeteners

The best honey, nutritionally speaking, comes from local bees. For this reason, you should try to find a keeper in your area. Honey should be unfiltered, unpasteurized, and mild-flavored so that it doesn't challenge the flavor of the carob in the recipe.

Other acceptable sweeteners include maple syrup, unsulphured molasses (rarely used as the *total* sweetener in a recipe because of its pronounced flavor), barley malt syrup, sorghum, and rice syrup. Avoid fructose and "powdered honey" with suspicion until all the research results are in.

Avoid, too, "buttered" or "creamed" honeys. These are usually processed honeys with the crystal seeds put back in. To increase their shelf-life, most processed honeys are heated under pressure and forced through multiple filters. Some packers then add silica to help filter out the nutritious particles that cause granulation—a perfectly natural process. By this time, most of the nutrients and enzymes have been destroyed or diluted and important substances, such as pollen, which should abound in honey, become nonexistent.

If the honey you bought is the real thing, it will have a delicate taste and aroma, a slightly cloudy appearance, and a tendency to crystallize not long after purchase.

But perhaps *most* indispensable to the natural baker is date sugar (not a sugar at all, but just granulated dried dates). The price is high but well worth it. Although date sugar is less sweet and lacks the dissolving properties of table sugar, it can be substituted for the refined sucrose in your baked goods at least half of the time. Stock some!

Storing

Use airtight jars or tins, because these sweeteners evaporate when they are exposed to the air. They do not need to be refrigerated and will last indefinitely. Edible honey has been found in 3,000-year-old Egyptian tombs, so don't worry about honey's staying power.

Honey and maple syrup can harden (it's called "sugaring"). However, this does not mean that the sweetener is spoiled. It can be reliquefied by placing the jar in a pan of warm water and heating slowly over low heat. Do not heat the honey over 115 degrees Fahrenheit, because high temperatures will destroy the honey's enzymes.

A mold may form over the surface of maple syrup, but this does not mean that the syrup is spoiled. Simply scrape the mold off and reliquefy the syrup to restore its original flavor and consistency. Store molasses in an airtight container in a cool, dry place. You may find that you use less of this sweetener and, therefore, will not have to keep a lot on hand.

Making Your Own Sugar-Free Sweeteners

None of the following are substitutes for granulated or confectioners' sugar. They are considerably less sweet, like carob, but they make excellent low-potency sweeteners and help to reduce the amount of full-strength sweetener normally used. They also make good substitutes for grated chocolate and cereal and tea sweeteners.

Homemade Fruit Sugars (Real Fructose)

1. *Citrus Sugar.* Peel any unwaxed, unsprayed ripe citrus fruit (tangelos, kumquats, tangerines, mandarin oranges, as well as oranges, lemons, and grapefruit). Dry the peels at room temperature for 2 days, or until they are almost brittle. Grind the dried peels in a blender or spice mill. Store the sugar in a tightly covered jar.

2. *Apple Sugar.* Save the unblemished peels from

unwaxed, unsprayed apples. Desiccate in a food dryer, or let them dry naturally in a warm room, or under a hot sun until crumbly (but not brittle). Grind to a powder in a spice mill or crush between 2 sheets of wax paper. Store in a tightly covered jar. For *apple-cinnamon fructose,* pulverize half a cinnamon stick in a spice mill or blender with 1 cup tightly packed peels.

3. *All-Grain Sugar.* Sprout whole barley, soft wheat, or hard wheat kernels for 3 days. Dry them in a low (150-degree) oven until you can grind them. Pulverize this sweet powder and store in small airtight jars in a cool place. For *grain-fruit sugar,* combine equal parts of one of the fruit sugars with grain sugar.

Sweeteners

Homemade Vanilla Extract (Non-Alcoholic)

1. Cut up a vanilla bean and cover it with ¼ cup boiling water. Cover the bowl and let it steep overnight.

2. Grind the mixture in a blender and strain the mixture, reserving the vanilla pulp.*

3. Add ½ teaspoon liquid or granulated lecithin and 1 tablespoon each of unrefined vegetable oil and honey to the strained liquid. Pour into a screw-top jar and refrigerate. Shake well before using. Use slightly more than you would commercial vanilla extract.

---

*Do not discard the strained-off pulp. Use 2 tablespoons of it in your next cake or batch of brownies for 1 tablespoon of the called-for liquid sweetener.

Homemade Vanilla Extract (Alcoholic)

This has to mature for three months. The longer it sits, the better the flavor.

1. Put 1 or 2 cut-up vanilla beans into a pint of inexpensive brandy. Cap the bottle tightly and let sit for at least 4 weeks, but preferably 12.

2. When half the contents of the brandy bottle are gone, start another batch.

The Spice Capsule

The first thing you must remember when you shop for spices and herbs is to invest in only the best. Leaves last longer than powdered spices, but not forever, so buy in small quantities. All spices, with the exception of turmeric, cardamom, and possibly cinnamon, should be ground as needed.

Flavoring Agents

Here are some new seasoning ideas for you to try when you cook or bake those old favorites of yours. How about adding fresh or dried carnation petals or a splash of rosewater instead of cinnamon? Dried fiddlehead ferns instead of pumpkin seeds? You can substitute lemon balm or lemon verbena for lemon peel or lemon juice. You can sprinkle toasted alfalfa on your green peas. Ground allspice can do the job for cloves and nutmeg, and borage can replace parsley. Chamomile is a good substitute for apple flavoring in anything you bake or stew. Angelica gives a dish a pleasant parsley-celery flavor, and bergamot mimics lemon. Don't overlook hibiscus for a tart all-purpose fruity flavor or toasted, ground fenugreek seeds when you're out of vanilla or maple extract.

And, here's a little tip that might surprise you: To increase the potency of any spice, extract, or herb, add a few pinches of freshly ground black pepper to the mixture in your bowl or pot and stir away.

Sprinkles, Candy Coatings, and Dusting Powders

When a recipe calls for rolling, dusting, coating, or sprinkling your homemade carob candies or baked goods, here are some tasty alternatives to the usual granulated or confectioners' sugar and chocolate "sprinkles." These can be used with or without a glaze on your baked goods, but they should always be applied while the doughnuts or cupcakes are still warm. To use as "sugars," spoon the ingredients into a paper bag and add the baked goods, two at a time, shaking until they are coated. To use as "sprinkles" or sugars, spread the ingredients on a sheet of wax paper. Dip the frosted or glazed portion of each goody into the powder. Or, you can simply sprinkle the powder on top of the glaze. Soft, shaped candies can be rolled in these mixtures.

- Unsweetened flaked coconut, toasted or raw
- Oven-roasted rolled oats
- Raw or lightly toasted and coarsely ground sprouts, seeds, or nuts
- Date sugar
- Dried, ground peel of organic oranges, tangerines, lemons, or any citrus fruit
- Toasted millet or toasted sesame, chia, or poppy seeds (use with a glaze only)
- Dried finely pulverized vanilla beans mixed with wheat germ
- Crushed granola or toasted rolled oats

- Wheat germ, corn germ, or bran flakes
- Pumpkin or sunflower seed meal
- Finely diced dried fruit
- Bee pollen or lecithin granules (make a melted "butter bud glaze" by sprinkling pollen over any hot glaze)
- Powdered herbs/tea leaves (try aromatic blends, such as peppermint and chamomile, rose hips and cinnamon, lemon balm and alfalfa, alone or with any of the other combinations listed
- Apricot, peach, or nectarine kernels (for an almond extract flavor)
- Bioflavonoid powder (save the white pith from under the peel of citrus fruits; dry at room temperature and crush or grind to a powder; mix with carob powder)
- Unseasoned (without salt or sugar) puffed cereals, crushed granola, or muesli-type cereals
- Vanilla-bean scented dry milk powder (make by burying a split vanilla bean in a jar of dry milk powder)
- Crushed sugar-free cookies or graham crackers
- Dry milk powder sifted with one part carob powder plus 1 teaspoon freshly ground white or black pepper
- Mock licorice (made by grinding together 2 teaspoons ground cinnamon, ½ teaspoon fennel seed, and ½ teaspoon whole cloves; stir spice mixture into 1 cup dry milk powder; Szechuan pepper and star anise can also be added
- Sugar 'n' Spice (made by combining ¾ cup finely ground date sugar with ¼ teaspoon ground mace); 1 teaspoon wheat germ plus 1 teaspoon soy granules or carob meal can also be added
- Coconut confetti (made by putting raw unsweetened

flaked or finely ground coconut into three bowls and tossing with beet, pomegranate, cherry, or strawberry juice *for red,* blueberry juice *for blue,* and strong chamomile tea or saffron broth *for yellow;* dry and mix the colored coconuts together)
● Carob-plus powder (made by mixing small amounts of ground ginger, ground pumpkin pie spice, dry milk powder, or aromatic tea herbs with carob)

Guidelines for Other Ingredients

1. In general, opt for whole foods (i.e., whole wheat, peanuts with skins, undegerminated corn, etc.) that have been freshly ground (i.e., flour and peanut butter), freshly picked, or freshly packed. Look for unrefined oils sold in cans or dark bottles.

2. Use organic produce as often as your budget allows.

3. Use local produce from local farmers and dairies, rather than produce that has been flown or shipped from other parts of the country.

4. Avoid salt. Instead, use powdered kelp or ascorbate powder (which is also available as calcium ascorbate). In this way you will add vitamin C plus minerals. When this is not possible, choose the low-sodium versions of such staples as baking powder (which should also be aluminum-free) and soy sauce.

Using the Pod

Carob in its natural state is chewy-sweet and fibrous. It is soft, but with a delicacy and subtlety that "natural" chocolate, handicapped by its tannic bitterness, lacks.

Eaten as it is to combat diarrhea, dysentery, or digestive disorders, or as a protein-mineral supplement, carob is a taste-terrific candy bar substitute that requires no wrapping, no refrigeration, no forethought, and no regrets.

Roasting and Storing

1. Whole pods may be eaten raw or dry-roasted in a low (300 degree) oven just before eating to increase their palatability. (But don't eat the seeds; they can be toxic.)

2. The pods may be roasted before or after grinding if you are converting them to a powder or meal. (You will find it easier to grind roasted pods.) By manipulating roasting times and oven temperatures up or down, you can produce three distinct "roasts," from light to medium to a deep espresso, coffee-colored shade. You must remember, though, that while roasting improves the flavor, heat destroys the nutrients. So, aim for a light brown roast for the best flavor and maximum nutritional value.

Note: 2 pounds of whole pods will yield approximately 2 cups of powder. High-fiber powders will yield slightly more.

3. Whole carob pods are long shelf-life foods, but nothing keeps forever. Store the pods under conditions that are neither too dry nor too humid. And wrap them well. If the pods are stored in the refrigerator for more than a few weeks, they will become very brittle. Storing them in a very warm place will also make them brittle. To soften a batch of brittle pods, steam them over boiling water or roast them in a low-temperature oven.

Making Carob Meal or Grits

Note: Carob has a tendency to clog grinders, so pass the pods through twice, slowly.

1. Oven-roast the pods. Break the pods with pliers and extract the seeds.

2. Pass the broken pods through a grinder or food mill to produce a gritty, high-fiber meal. Use the meal to add a chocolate flavor to beverages, candies, or baked goods. Carob is also a nutrition booster, supplying a generous amount of many nutrients, especially calcium, pectin, and the B vitamins.

3. Store the ground carob in an airtight container in a cool place.

For added fiber and a higher nutrient value, stir in 2 tablespoons raw or toasted wheat or corn bran or wheat germ to your batch of ground carob.

Making Carob Powder

Method 1: Put the washed pods in a pressure cooker at 15 pounds pressure and cook for 20 minutes. When cool, split the pods open and remove the seeds. (Wear rubber gloves so you don't stain your hands.) Cut the pods into small pieces and put them on a baking sheet. Dry the pod pieces in a very low oven (150 degrees). Put the dried pods in the container of a food processor or blender and grind to a coarse meal. (You can also put the dried pods through a grinder.) Blend the coarse meal into a finer powder. Use the powder raw or roast it before using.

Method 2: Break open each dry pod with pliers and remove the seeds. Roast the pods slowly in a very low oven (150 degrees) for 15 to 20 minutes. Cool. Grind in a stone grinder at a coarse setting. Grind again at a finer setting.

Method 3: Wash the pods thoroughly and cover them with boiling water. Let stand about 15 minutes, or until softened. Drain, cool, and cut along the seam side of the pod to extract the seeds. (Wear rubber gloves so you don't stain your hands.) Cut the pods into small pieces and dry out-of-doors under a hot sun for 3 to 4 hours. (You can also dry the cut-up pods in a very low oven [150 degrees].) Put through a grinder or blend two or three times. Sift out any large pieces before using the powder.

Note: For a high-fiber powder, stir back into the fine powder the large granular bits left in the sifter.

Using Block Carob, Carob Bars, and Carob Chips

These are the least acceptable forms of carob because they are the most processed. In addition to the refined sugar, which, at this writing, is present in 99 percent of the solid baking carob available, there may be other questionable sugars present in the form of lactose, fructose, dextrose, and sorbitol, as well as objectionable stabilizers and emulsifiers.

Before you buy any of these products, read labels and ask questions. You just may discover a supply of the no-sugar or low-sugar versions which are beginning to appear on the market. In any case, remember that carob is naturally sweet and that there is no carobic equivalent of bitter or unsweetened cocoa or chocolate. (You can produce homemade taste-alike substitutes in syrup form by using the powder-based recipes in this book.)

Carob blocks and chips should be well wrapped and refrigerated. They may also be frozen. Keep for only 6 to 12 months.

Grating

The carob block should be at room temperature. Use a Mouli grater, a flat or standing hand grater, or a blender or food processor. (If using the blender or food processor, you will have to chop the block into small pieces.)

Shavings and Curls

The carob block should be firm and at room temperature or slightly warmer. Make shavings with a sharp swivel-bladed vegetable peeler. For *large curls,* carefully draw a swivel-bladed vegetable peeler across the broad, flat side of the block. For *small curls,* draw the peeler across the thin, edge side of the block, using long strokes to produce larger curls. Avoid breaking the fragile curls by lifting and moving them with a wooden toothpick.

Melting

There are three methods for melting carob.

1. Break the carob block into small pieces or use chips. Put the carob in a small heavy-bottomed pan. Put the pan in a preheated oven which has been turned off. The residual heat in the oven will melt the carob. You can also melt the carob in a microwave oven set for 90 seconds.

2. Put the carob pieces in the top of a double boiler over hot, not boiling, water. Stir until melted and smooth.

3. Carob can also be melted over direct heat, with patient stirring, if the pan rests on an asbestos pad or Flame-Tamer. This method is the least preferred.

Using the Powder or Flour

Carob powder can be purchased raw or roasted, sweetened or unsweetened. Sweetening carob is like gilding a lily, because carob is about half as sweet as sugar.

What's the difference between raw and roasted carob? It is largely one of taste, not nutrition (unless the powder is extremely dark, which signals destruction of essential nutrients). Lightly roasted carob powder does taste better. For optimum taste and optimum nutrition, buy the plastic bags or boxes of raw carob that are packaged by your health food store and dry-roast the carob yourself in a dry heavy skillet or in a low (150-degree) oven.

Note: When substituting carob powder for other flours, lower your oven temperature by 25 degrees to prevent burning. Also, if you are *adding,* not substituting, carob, remember you are adding *sweetening* powder as well.

Storing

Because powdered carob has hygroscopic properties (meaning it attracts moisture), it should be stored in a tightly closed container or in a screw-top jar in a cool, dry place. You can bring lumpy carob powder back to usefulness by crushing it, then sifting out the lumps.

Carob Syrups

Carob syrup is absolutely delicious in both its cocoa-brown and pale-gold versions. It is about as thick as honey, and priced about a third higher. It is available in many health food stores and in the nutritional sections of supermarkets.

Creating Your Own Carob Syrups

Unsweetened Carob Syrup

This syrup can be used as a substitute for bitter or unsweetened chocolate.

1 cup unsweetened carob powder
1 cup water
2 tablespoons unsalted butter (optional)

Mix the carob powder, water, and butter in a small saucepan. Bring to a boil over very low heat. Lower the heat and simmer for 5 to 8 minutes, or until the syrup is smooth. Cool, pour into a screw-top jar, and refrigerate.

Makes 1¼ cups.

Semisweet Carob Syrup

Follow the recipe for Unsweetened Carob Syrup, but before simmering add ¼ cup honey (or to taste) and 1 to 2 tablespoons unsalted butter or unrefined vegetable oil.

Sweetened Carob Syrup

Spoon this syrup over yogurt, plain ice cream, ice cream sundaes, banana splits, or vanilla pudding.

1   **cup sifted unsweetened carob powder**
1   **tablespoon arrowroot or cornstarch**
¼   **cup honey**
1½ **cups water**
2   **teaspoons pure vanilla extract**

Combine the carob powder and arrowroot in a saucepan. Gradually add the honey and water. Put the pan on a Flame-Tamer and bring the liquid to a boil. Lower the heat and simmer gently for 5 minutes, stirring frequently with a wire whisk. Remove from the heat and cool for 5 minutes. Stir in the vanilla. Cool completely, pour into a screw-top jar, and refrigerate.

Makes 2 cups.

Desweetened Carob Syrup

This is a bittersweet syrup, somewhat similar to unsweetened melted chocolate.

1   **cup strong decaffeinated coffee, herb coffee, or dandelion tea**
¼   **cup unsweetened carob chips or unsweetened block carob, broken into small pieces**
½   **whole vanilla bean, cut into 4 pieces with a scissor**

Combine all the ingredients in the top of a double boiler. Bring to a boil over simmering water, stirring constantly. Remove from the heat as soon as the proper syrup consistency is reached. Remove the vanilla bean pieces. Cool the syrup, pour into a screw-top jar, and refrigerate.

Makes 1 cup

Note: You can give any of the above syrups a bit more stability by stirring in 1 slightly beaten egg white after the syrups have cooled.

Carob for Coating

Melt block carob or broken carob candy bars in a heavy saucepan over low heat. Or put the carob pieces in the top of a double boiler over hot, not boiling, water and stir until melted. Stir in 1 teaspoon liquid lecithin (or the contents of a lecithin capsule) and blend well.

Stir the melted carob to keep it glossy and dip in chopped fruits, roasted nuts, large sprouted beans, etc., using a skewer, knitting needle, demitasse spoon, or chopsticks to hold the food to be coated. Put the coated food on wax paper. Chill. These dipped confections may be frozen for long periods of time in airtight containers.

4
Recipes

In the recipes that follow, the term "carob syrup" refers to any one of the homemade syrups on pages 31–33, bearing in mind that each differs in its ability to sweeten the chosen recipe. You may also use either of the two commercial types of carob syrup (light or dark) as well.

Remember that the carob powder called for in the recipes is *always* unsweetened.

Vegetarian Entrees

Mock Beef Bretonne

---

4 tablespoons unsalted butter or unrefined vegetable oil
3 pounds tofu, drained and cubed
1 clove garlic, peeled and crushed
3 medium-sized onions, peeled and sliced
4 tablespoons unbleached flour
½ cup dry red wine
½ cup water
2 teaspoons kelp
½ teaspoon freshly ground black pepper
¼ teaspoon crushed dried rosemary
¼ teaspoon dried oregano, crushed
1 cup unsweetened carob cocoa
   Whole kumquats or navel orange slices and fresh mint sprigs for garnish

1. Melt the butter in a deep frying pan. Add the cubed tofu and brown on all sides. Remove to a plate with a slotted spoon.

2. Add the garlic and onions to the fat in the frying pan and sauté until the onions are soft but not brown. Remove the garlic and onions with a slotted spoon and add to the browned tofu.

3. Blend the flour with the fat remaining in the frying pan. Add the wine, water, kelp, pepper, rosemary, oregano, and cocoa to the frying pan. Stir over medium heat until slightly thickened.

4. Return the tofu and onions to the frying pan and mix in well. Bring to a boil, cover, lower the heat,

---

and simmer for 30 minutes. Garnish with whole kumquats, or surround with orange slices and fresh mint sprigs before serving.

Makes 6 servings.

Meatless Cheeseburger Pie

3 **cups ground raw mushrooms**
2 **cups soft whole-wheat bread crumbs**
2 **eggs**
½ **cup unsweetened carob syrup**
½ **cup heavy cream**
2 **tablespoons minced onion**
1 **teaspoon soy sauce**
1 **tablespoon dry mustard**
4 **slices mild Cheddar cheese**

1. Combine the mushrooms, bread crumbs, and eggs in a large bowl. Add the carob syrup, cream, and minced onion and mix in well. Let sit for 10 minutes. Add the soy sauce and mustard and mix well.

2. Preheat the oven to 350 degrees.

3. Press the mushroom mixture into a buttered 10-inch pie dish. Bake for 35 minutes.

4. Remove the pie dish from the oven. Cut the cheese slices in half diagonally and arrange them over the top of the pie.

5. Put the dish under the broiler until the cheese melts and turns brown.

Makes 6 to 8 servings.

Carob Baked Beans

1 medium-sized onion, peeled
2 pounds cooked pinto, pink or navy beans, partially drained
½ teaspoon dry mustard
  Sea salt
  Freshly ground black pepper
¼ cup unsweetened carob syrup
½ cup carob cocoa
½ cup boiling water
1 teaspoon meat-free broth paste
2 tablespoons wheat germ flakes

1. Preheat the oven to 350 degrees.

2. Combine the onions, beans, and dry mustard in a bean pot or deep casserole. Season with salt and pepper to taste.

3. Combine the carob syrup, cocoa, water, and broth paste and pour over the beans.

4. Bake for 40 minutes. Sprinkle the wheat germ flakes over the top of the beans and bake for 20 minutes longer.

Makes 6 to 8 servings.

Cara-Carob Cabbage

6 cups finely shredded red cabbage
¼ cup carob syrup or honey
2 tablespoons unsalted butter (optional)
¼ cup lemon juice

½ teaspoon salt, or to taste

½ teaspoon caraway seeds

    1. Steam the cabbage over simmering water for 5 minutes.

    2. Preheat the oven to 300 degrees.

    3. Combine the cabbage with the remaining ingredients in an oven-proof casserole. Bake for ½ hour, or until the flavors are well blended. Serve hot.

Makes 8 servings.

Carob-Glazed Yams

  4 large yams

    Unsalted butter

    Ground cinnamon (optional)

    Unsweetened carob syrup

    Sesame seeds

    1. Preheat the oven to 350 degrees.

    2. Scrub the yams with a stiff-bristled brush under cool running water. (You will have to peel the yams if they have been treated with wax.)

    3. Slice the yams ⅜ inch thick. Make layers of the yam slices in a baking dish, dotting each layer generously with butter and sprinkling on cinnamon, if you wish. Drizzle a small amount of carob syrup over the top of the yams and sprinkle some sesame seeds over the syrup.

    4. Bake for 45 to 60 minutes, or until soft.

Makes 8 servings.

Fudge Noodles

If you love fruit soup, try adding some of these noodles the next time you serve it.

- **3 eggs**
- **3 tablespoons cold water**
- **3 tablespoons unsweetened carob powder**
- **Unrefined vegetable oil**

1. Beat the eggs until frothy. Blend in the water and carob powder thoroughly.

2. Heat a small, heavy frying pan and brush it with oil. Pour in 1 tablespoon of the batter and tilt the pan to distribute it evenly. Cook over moderate heat until brown on both sides. Remove the browned pancake to a plate and continue making pancakes until all the batter has been used.

3. When the pancakes are cool, roll them up and slice them into thin noodles. Serve with hot fruit soups or as an accompaniment to sweet and sour dishes.

Makes 4 servings.

Vegetarian Mole

Serve this peppery sauce over vegetarian tamales, stuffed peppers, or Mexican-style polenta.

- **½ pound sweet red peppers**
- **½ pound sweet green peppers**
- **3 hot red peppers, or 2 ounces red pepper flakes**
- **Unrefined vegetable oil**

1   clove garlic, peeled and chopped
1   small onion, peeled and chopped
¼   pound tomatoes, cored and cut into wedges
8   whole black peppercorns, crushed
½   cinnamon stick
1   teaspoon ground cumin
1   small ripe banana, peeled and diced
1   slice toasted bread, cubed
1   tablespoon yellow cornmeal
2   ounces slivered almonds
2   ounces raw peanuts
2   ounces currants
4   cups vegetable broth, or as needed
6   tablespoons unsweetened carob powder

1. Cut the peppers in half, remove the seeds and membranes, and slice.

2. Heat 3 tablespoons of the oil in a large frying pan. Add the sliced peppers and sauté until just tender, about 5 minutes. Remove the peppers with a slotted spoon and set them aside.

3. Add the garlic to the oil in the frying pan and sauté for 1 minute. Then add the onion, tomatoes, peppercorns, cinnamon stick, cumin, diced banana, bread cubes, cornmeal, almonds, peanuts, and currants. Sauté for about 5 minutes, adding more oil if necessary so the mixture doesn't burn. Cool slightly.

4. Put the peppers and the vegetable-spice mixture into the container of a blender and blend to a paste. Add vegetable broth to thin the paste to the desired consistency.

5. Pour the sauce into a saucepan and stir in 3 tablespoons of the carob powder. Heat the sauce over low heat. Taste and gradually stir in the remaining carob powder as desired.

Makes 5 cups.

Cakes, Cookies, Pies

Carob Fruit Cake

Wrap this cake in cheesecloth that has been soaked in cider or sweet wine, and store it in an airtight tin for several weeks. You will find that the flavor improves with time. For extra flavor, drizzle on some melted carob before serving.

1	**cup unsalted butter, softened**
1½	**cups honey**
3	**cups plus 2 tablespoons unbleached flour**
½	**cup unsweetened carob powder**
2	**teaspoons baking powder**
2	**teaspoons baking soda**
½	**teaspoon ground mace**
½	**teaspoon ground cinnamon**
4	**eggs**
¾	**cup apple cider**
2	**cups figs, finely minced**
1	**cup pitted dates, finely minced**
2	**cups raisins**
1	**cup currants**
1	**teaspoon grated orange peel**
1	**cup chopped nuts**

1. Preheat the oven to 300 degrees.

2. Beat the butter and honey together until fluffy.

3. Sift together the 3 cups flour, carob powder, baking powder, baking soda, mace, and cinnamon.

4. Add the dry ingredients to the creamed mixture, alternately with the eggs. Beat well after each addition. Stir in the cider.

5. Sprinkle the remaining 2 tablespoons of flour over the figs, dates, raisins, and currants. Toss to coat the fruits well. Add the fruits, orange rind, and nuts to the batter and stir to blend in.

6. Pour into a large buttered and floured Bundt pan and bake for 2 hours, or until a toothpick inserted in the center comes out clean.

Makes 18 servings.

Sacher Torte

½   **cup unsweetened carob syrup**
2   **tablespoons honey**
¼   **cup unsalted butter**
4   **egg yolks**
½   **teaspoon pure vanilla extract**
6   **egg whites**
3   **tablespoons honey, warmed**
¾   **cup whole-wheat pastry flour**
½   **cup Carob-Cherry Icing (see page 80)**
     Hot Carob Dribble (see page 79)
1   **cup heavy cream, whipped (optional)**

    1. Preheat the oven to 350 degrees.

    2. In a small saucepan, heat the carob syrup and 2 tablespoons honey, stirring until smooth. Add the butter and stir until the butter melts. Do not let the mixture boil. Remove from the heat and cool.

3. In a small bowl, beat the egg yolks very lightly with a fork. Beat in the cooled carob mixture and the vanilla.

4. In a large bowl, beat the egg whites until foamy. Gradually beat in the 3 tablespoons of warmed honey, about a teaspoon at a time, beating until the whites are stiff.

5. Mix 1 cup of the beaten whites into the yolk mixture and fold the yolk mixture into the remaining whites.

6. Sift the flour over the egg white mixture and fold it in thoroughly. Do not overblend.

7. Pour into two 9-inch cake pans which have been buttered and lined with wax paper. Bake for 20 to 25 minutes.

8. Turn cakes out onto wire racks and remove wax paper. Cool completely.

9. Put one cooled layer on a rack which has been set over a tray. Spread evenly with the Carob-Cherry Icing. Top with the second layer. Spread the Hot Carob Dribble evenly over the sides and top of the torte. Transfer the torte to a serving platter and refrigerate for several hours to harden the frosting.

10. Allow the torte to come to room temperature before serving. Garnish each piece with whipped cream, if you wish.

Makes 8 servings.

Cinnamon Rose Cake

3 cups pastry flour

1 teaspoon ground cinnamon, ground dried rose petals, or rosewater

½ teaspoon ground cloves

2 teaspoons baking soda

1 cup shortening

2 cups date sugar

2 eggs

2 cups raw, pared and chopped apples

1 cup chopped nuts or raisins

1 cup cold double-strength carob cocoa

1. Preheat the oven to 350 degrees.

2. Sift together the flour, cinnamon, cloves, and baking soda and set aside.

3. Cream the shortening with the sugar until light and fluffy. Add the eggs one at a time, beating well after each addition. Stir in the apples and nuts.

4. Add the sifted dry ingredients to the creamed mixture alternately with the cocoa, mixing well after each addition.

5. Pour the batter into a buttered 9- x 13-inch baking pan and bake for 45 to 60 minutes.

Makes 12 servings.

Carob-Zucchini Cake

2½ cups whole-wheat flour
2½ teaspoons baking powder
1½ teaspoons baking soda
 ½ cup unsweetened carob powder
 1 teaspoon ground cinnamon
 ¾ cup butter, softened
 2 teaspoons pure vanilla extract
 2 cups finely shredded zucchini
 2 cups honey
 3 eggs
 ⅓ cup milk

1. Preheat the oven to 350 degrees.

2. Combine the flour, baking powder, baking soda, carob powder, and cinnamon together. Set aside.

3. In a large bowl, beat the butter, vanilla, zucchini, honey, eggs, and milk together for 3 minutes. Add the dry ingredients and mix to combine well.

4. Pour the batter into a buttered 9- x 13-inch baking pan. Bake for 35 to 40 minutes, or until a toothpick inserted in the center comes out clean. The cake may be frosted or glazed after it has cooled.

Makes 12 servings.

Variation: The batter may be spooned into greased cupcake tins and baked for about 25 minutes.

Gingerbread Cake

This carob fruitcake is good for all occasions. Because it keeps well, it is excellent for gift-giving.

1   cup hot water
1   cup carob syrup or honey
½   cup unsalted butter or nut oil
2   teaspoons baking soda
1   teaspoon baking powder
1   teaspoon pure vanilla extract
1½   teaspoons ground aniseed
1   teaspoon ground cinnamon
¾   teaspoon ground ginger
¼   teaspoon ground cloves
2   cups rye flour
1¼   cups unbleached flour
¼   cup carob powder
1   teaspoon grated orange peel
⅔   cup chopped blanched almonds
½   cup currants or finely chopped raisins

1. Preheat the oven to 400 degrees.

2. In a large bowl, pour the hot water over the carob syrup and butter or oil. Add the baking soda and baking powder and stir to dissolve. Add the vanilla, aniseed, cinnamon, ginger, cloves, and 1 cup of each of the flours. Stir to blend well. Add the remaining flour and carob powder and stir to make a thick, smooth batter. Add the orange peel, almonds, and currants and stir just to incorporate them into the batter. Do not overblend. Set the batter aside while preparing the pans.

3. Butter three 6½- x 3½-inch loaf pans. Line the sides but not the bottoms of the pans with wax paper, leaving a 1-inch collar all around the top edges of the pans. (This collar will make it easier to remove the loaves after they are baked.)

4. Pour the batter into the prepared pans until they are three quarters full. Put the pans on the middle shelf of the oven. Bake for 10 minutes. Lower the oven temperature to 350 degrees, and bake for 50 minutes. The loaves should rise about 1 inch above the pans and be a deep golden brown when baked. There should be a large crevice running the length of each loaf.

5. Remove the loaves from the oven and tug on the paper collars to free the loaves from the pan. Cool the loaves on wire racks. When cool, wrap the loaves tightly in aluminum foil or in plastic bags and let age for several days.

Makes 3 loaves.

Basic "Not-Chocolate" Cupcakes

3 cups whole-grain flour
½ cup unsweetened carob powder
1 teaspoon kelp or ascorbate powder (optional)
¼ teaspoon "dusting powder" (see The Spice Capsule, page 22) or ground nutmeg
3 teaspoons baking soda
1 cup softened unsalted butter or unrefined vegetable oil
1 cup date sugar
3 egg yolks
1 teaspoon fragrant herbs (see The Spice Capsule, page 22)
2 cups sour cream or plain yogurt

1. Preheat the oven to 300 degrees.

2. Sift together the flour, carob powder, kelp, "dusting powder," and baking soda. Set aside.

3. Beat the butter and sugar together until creamy and fluffy. Add the egg yolks and herbs and beat well.

4. Add the dry ingredients and sour cream alternately to the creamed mixture, beating well after each addition.

5. Butter 36 cupcake tins and fill them two-thirds full with the batter. Bake for 25 to 30 minutes.

Makes 36 cupcakes.

Carob Crullers

2 packages (¼ ounce each) active dry yeast
¼ cup warm water
1½ cups lukewarm scalded milk
¼ cup honey
2 scant tablespoons unsweetened carob powder
1 teaspoon ground nutmeg
¼ teaspoon ground cinnamon
2 eggs
⅓ cup unrefined vegetable oil
4½ cups pastry flour
½ cup melted unsalted butter

1. Put the yeast and water in a large mixing bowl. Let sit for 5 minutes so that the yeast dissolves.

2. Stir in the milk, honey, carob powder, nutmeg, cinnamon, eggs, oil, and 2 cups of the flour. Beat on low speed with an electric mixer for ½ minute, scraping the sides of the bowl constantly.

3. Beat for 2 minutes on medium speed, scraping the sides of the bowl occasionally. Stir in the remaining flour until the dough is smooth.

4. Cover the bowl with a damp cloth and let the dough rise in a warm place for 50 to 60 minutes, or until it has doubled in bulk.

5. Turn the dough out onto a well-floured, cloth-covered board. Roll the dough around lightly to coat it with flour. (The dough will be soft.) Roll the dough out to a ½-inch thickness using a floured, cloth-covered rolling pin. Cut with a floured 2½-inch doughnut cutter.

6. Twist each doughnut into a cruller and put the

shaped crullers on a buttered baking sheet. Brush with melted butter. Let rise for 20 minutes, or until doubled.

7. Preheat the oven to 425 degrees.

8. Bake the crullers for 8 to 10 minutes, or until brown and firm. Brush immediately with melted butter.

Makes 2 dozen crullers.

Variations: Dust the crullers with a mixture from The Spice Capsule (page 22).

The carob powder may be omitted from the batter and combined with cinnamon, nutmeg, or homemade fruit sugar and dusted over the hot crullers.

Spud Nuts

1   **cup milk**
2   **tablespoons honey**
1   **teaspoon salt (optional)**
¼   **cup unsalted butter**
1   **package active dry yeast**
¼   **cup warm (105 to 115 degrees) water**
¾   **cup unseasoned mashed potatoes**
2   **eggs**
5   **cups sifted whole-wheat pastry flour**
¼   **cup unsweetened carob powder**
    Unrefined vegetable oil for frying

1. Heat the milk in a small saucepan until bubbles form around the sides of the pan. Remove from the heat and add the honey, salt, and butter. Stir until the butter has melted. Let cool to lukewarm.

2. In a large bowl, sprinkle the yeast over the warm water (if possible, check the temperature of the water with a thermometer). Stir until the yeast has dissolved.

3. Add the lukewarm milk mixture, mashed potatoes, eggs, and 2 cups of the flour to the yeast. Beat at medium speed on an electric mixer until the dough is smooth, about 2 minutes.

4. Beat in the remaining flour with a wooden spoon. Beat until the dough is smooth. Cover the bowl with a damp towel and let rise in a warm place until doubled.

5. Punch the dough down and turn it out onto a well-floured pastry cloth. Turn the dough to coat it with flour. Knead 10 times, or until the dough is smooth and elastic.

6. Cover the dough with a bowl and let it rest for 10 minutes.

7. Roll the dough out to a ½-inch thickness on a floured pastry cloth. Cut with a 3-inch doughnut cutter. Use a wide spatula to move the doughnuts to the edge of the pastry cloth.

8. Gather the scraps of dough into a ball, reroll, and cut into doughnut shapes. Cover the doughnuts with a damp towel and let rise for 45 minutes.

9. Pour 1½ to 2 inches of oil into an electric skillet or heavy saucepan and heat to 375 degrees.

10. Gently drop 3 or 4 doughnuts at a time into the hot oil. When the doughnuts rise to the surface, turn them over. Fry until golden brown on both sides, about 3 minutes. Drain well and glaze.

Makes 2 dozen.

Cubby Holes

These are cake-type baked doughnuts without holes.

2 cups whole-wheat or unbleached flour
2 teaspoons baking powder
¼ teaspoon ground mace
¼ teaspoon ground cinnamon
4 tablespoons honey
4 tablespoons softened unsalted butter or creamy peanut butter
1 egg
½ cup carob cocoa
½ cup melted unsalted butter
½ cup dusting powder (see page 23)

1. Sift the flour, baking powder, mace, and cinnamon together and set aside.

2. Cream the honey, butter, and egg together until fluffy. Add the dry ingredients to the creamed mixture, alternating with the cocoa. Mix well after each addition.

3. Turn the dough out onto a lightly floured surface and knead it for 1 minute, adding more flour, if necessary, to make a soft but not sticky dough. Roll the dough out to a ⅓-inch thickness and cut with a 3-inch doughnut cutter.

4. Preheat the oven to 400 degrees.

5. Dip the doughnuts in the melted butter and then in the dusting powder and then ½ inch apart on a lightly buttered baking sheet.

6. Bake in the upper third of the oven for 15 to

20 minutes, or until browned. Glaze and dust while warm.

Makes 2 dozen.

Variation: If you don't want to glaze the doughnuts, you can spice them in a low-calorie way with *liquid cinnamon.* Combine 1 teaspoon freshly ground cinnamon with ¼ cup boiling water. Stir and baste each doughnut while it is still hot.

Brownie Pointers

Before Baking

1. To make *Checkerboard Brownies,* make up any of the basic light-colored batters for cakes or cookies. Divide the batter in half. Add 2 tablespoons unsweetened carob syrup to one bowl, or enough syrup to darken the batter as desired. Pour the batters by tablespoons into a buttered square pan, alternating light and dark batter.

2. To make *Ribbon Brownies,* alternate layers of light and dark batters. The pattern will emerge when the cake is sliced.

3. To make *Marbleized Brownies,* use any light-colored cake batter, reserving ½ cup of the batter. Add ⅓ cup unsweetened carob syrup and 1 tablespoon unsweetened carob powder to the reserved batter. Pour the light-colored batter into a buttered square pan and swirl in the carob batter with a table knife.

4. To make *Self-Streuseled Brownies,* sprinkle the surface of half-baked brownies with a ½-inch-thick layer of undercooked homemade granola.

5. To make *Pebbleton Brownies,* moisten (but don't

soak) ½ cup rolled oats in milk or cream and scatter them evenly over the top of the brownie dough before baking.

After Baking

Top your brownies with either of the following for an extra treat.

Brownie Dribble I

This is also good when spread on cupcakes or coffee cakes.

1 cup plain fresh yogurt
1 tablespoon unsweetened carob syrup
½ teaspoon pure vanilla extract

    1. Blend all the ingredients in a small bowl.
    2. Dribble over warm brownies and return the brownies to the turned-off oven for 10 minutes. Let the brownies cool. Refrigerate overnight before serving.

Brownie Dribble II

½ cup unsalted butter
6 ounces carob chips or block carob, grated
    Water or milk

    Combine the butter and carob chips in the top of a double boiler over hot, not boiling, water. Stir until melted. Add just enough water to thin the mixture to a dribbling consistency. Dribble over brownies and let set in or out of the refrigerator.

Sizes and Servings

1. An 8-inch round pan makes about 12 to 16 brownies.

2. An 8-inch square pan makes 6 to 10 big brownies.

3. A 9-inch square pan makes 10 large brownies

4. A 9- x 13- x 2-inch pan makes 24 brownies.

5. A 10-inch springform pan makes 12 to 14 brownies.

Textures and Baking Times

1. With special high-scorch-potential ingredients (soy flour, rice polish, etc.), bake in a 325-degree oven for 30 minutes.

2. For cake-like brownies, bake in a 350-degree oven for 30 to 45 minutes.

3. For moist, chewy brownies, bake in a 350-degree oven for 25 minutes.

4. For chewy brownies, add ½ to ¾ cup nuts, sprouts, or unsweetened flaked coconut to the brownie batter.

5. For the crunchiest brownies, add both unsweetened flaked coconut and slivered almonds to the brownie batter.

6. For really cake-like brownies, add rolled oats to the brownie batter.

Storing

Brownies (and most cookies) will keep crisper longer if stored in an airtight container which has crumpled tissue paper on the bottom.

Or you might try adding a few sugar cubes to the container. The sugar will absorb the moisture.

Cream Cheese Brownies

3 tablespoons unsalted butter
4 ounces block carob
¼ cup rose petals
2 tablespoons unrefined vegetable oil
3 ounces regular or low-fat cream cheese
¼ cup homemade sugar
3 eggs
1 tablespoon wheat germ
1 teaspoon ground dried orange or lemon peel
½ cup honey
½ cup unbleached flour
½ teaspoon baking powder
½ cup chopped walnuts
1 teaspoon pure vanilla extract
¼ teaspoon pure almond extract

1. Melt the butter and carob in the top of a double boiler over hot, not boiling, water. Set aside to cool.

2. Butter a 9-inch square baking pan and line it with fresh rose petals.

3. Preheat the oven to 350 degrees.

4. In a medium mixing bowl, cream the oil and cream cheese until fluffy. Beat in the sugar, 1 egg, the wheat germ, and the orange peel. Set aside.

5. In a large mixing bowl, beat the remaining eggs until foamy. Add the honey and beat until well blended. Stir in the flour and baking powder and blend well. Add the cool carob mixture, walnuts, and extracts.

6. Spread half the carob batter evenly in the prepared pan. Spread the cream cheese mixture on top. Drop spoonfuls of the remaining carob batter on top of the cream cheese mixture. Swirl the top of the batter slightly with a fork.

7. Bake for 40 to 50 minutes, or until the edges begin to pull away from the sides of the pan. Cool before cutting.

Makes 10 brownies.

Popcorn Brownies

These brownies are at their tastiest best when served warm.

½ **cup whole-wheat pastry flour**
1 **teaspoon baking powder**
⅓ **cup unsweetened carob powder**
½ **cup date sugar**
   Pinch of grated orange or lemon peel
½ **cup melted unsalted butter or unrefined vegetable oil**
½ **cup honey**
2 **eggs, well beaten**
½ **cup freshly popped popcorn, ground in a blender**
½ **cup chopped nuts or sprouts**

1. Preheat the oven to 350 degrees.

2. Sift the flour, baking powder, carob powder, sugar, and orange peel together. Set aside.

3. Combine the melted butter, honey, and eggs and mix well. Mix into the sifted dry ingredients. Add the ground popcorn and nuts and mix well.

4. Pour the batter into a buttered 8-inch square pan and bake for 40 minutes. Serve warm.

Makes 10 brownies.

Milky Whey Brownies

¾ **cup whey powder or dry milk powder**
¼ **cup arrowroot or unsweetened carob powder**
4 **to 5 tablespoons granola or crushed nuts**
Moist leaves from 1 used herb tea bag (such as chamomile, lemon verbena, or orangemint)
4 **to 5 tablespoons honey or unsweetened carob syrup**
Unsweetened carob powder

1. Mix the whey powder, arrowroot, and granola together in a small bowl. Add the moist tea leaves and enough honey to make a kneadable dough.

2. Dust a shallow candy dish with the carob powder and press the dough into the dish. Chill and cut into bars.

Makes 16 pieces.

Raw Brownies

1 **cup rolled oats**
½ **cup unsweetened carob powder**
¼ **cup ground toasted sesame seeds**
¼ **cup ground sunflower seeds**
½ **cup honey**
2 **cups chopped nuts**
1 **teaspoon any aromatic herb, such as peppermint, spearmint, or chamomile (optional)**

1. Combine all the ingredients in a medium-sized bowl.

2. Press the mixture into an 8-inch square dish. Chill.

3. Cut into bars or squares to serve.

Makes 16 pieces.

Variations: You may grind the oats to a powder for a finer texture. You may also substitute ground popcorn for the oats.

Oakies

3   tablespoons unsalted butter, softened
1   cup honey
½   teaspoon ascorbate powder or kelp (optional)
2   eggs
¼   cup okra or soybean pulp
1   teaspoon pure vanilla extract
¼   teaspoon baking soda
6   tablespoons unsweetened carob powder
3   teaspoons unrefined vegetable oil or melted unsalted butter
⅓   cup unbleached flour
1   tablespoon wheat germ
1   cup chopped nuts or chopped sprouts

1. Preheat the oven to 350 degrees.

2. Beat the butter and honey together until creamy. Add the ascorbate powder, eggs, okra, vanilla, and baking soda and blend well. Mix in the carob powder and oil and blend well. Add the flour, wheat germ, and chopped nuts and blend again.

3. Pour the batter into a buttered 8- or 9-inch square pan and bake for 30 to 45 minutes, or until desired texture is reached.

Makes 10 large brownies.

Carrot Brownies

2 cups pastry flour
½ cup wheat germ
1 teaspoon baking powder
½ teaspoon baking soda
½ cup unsalted butter, softened
¾ cup honey or less (carrots are sweet)
1 egg
2 cups carrot pulp*
3 tablespoons unsweetened carob powder
½ cup chopped walnuts (optional)

1. Preheat the oven to 350 degrees.

2. Sift the flour, wheat germ, baking powder, and baking soda together. Set aside.

3. Beat the butter and honey together until creamy. Add the egg and beat well.

4. Stir in the carob pulp and mix well. Sift the flour mixture and carob powder over the batter and mix in well. Stir in the walnuts.

5. Pour into a buttered 8- or 9-inch square pan and bake for 30 minutes.

Makes 10 large brownies.

*Grate carrots in your food processor and squeeze off any liquid to get the pulp. If you have a juice extractor, you will automatically get carrot pulp when you make carrot juice.

Swirled Mint Brownies

½ cup melted unsalted butter
½ cup honey
2 eggs
1 cup unbleached flour
½ teaspoon baking powder
¼ cup unsweetened carob syrup
½ teaspoon pure peppermint extract
   Several drops natural red coloring (use cranberry, strawberry, or beet juice)
   1. Preheat the oven to 350 degrees.
   2. In a medium-sized bowl, cream the butter and honey together until fluffy. Beat in the eggs.
   3. Combine the flour and baking powder and stir into the creamed mixture.
   4. Pour half the batter into another bowl. Stir the carob syrup into one half of the batter.
   5. Add the peppermint extract and enough natural coloring to make a medium pink to the other half of the dough.
   6. Drop each mixture by rounded tablespoons into a buttered 9- x 13-inch pan, alternating the batters to form a checkerboard pattern. Then gently swirl a spatula through the batter in a zigzag pattern to marbleize.
   7. Bake for 20 minutes. Cool before cutting. Serve plain or frosted.

Makes 24 brownies.

Solar Twinkies

1. Take any variety of whole-grain seeds (which have been plumped by soaking them in warm water for 48 hours) and drain and dry them.

2. Combine 1 part dried seeds, 2 parts pitted chopped dates, 1 part raisins, and 1 part chopped figs. Press through a food mill.

3. Knead enough unsweetened carob powder into the mixture so that the dough is not sticky. Roll out to a 1-inch thickness. Cut into squares and dry in the hot sun for 4 to 5 hours.

Carob Stars

¼ **cup boiling water**
6 **tablespoons unsweetened carob powder**
1 **cup unsalted butter, softened**
1 **teaspoon pure almond extract**
½ **cup homemade sugar or date sugar**
1 **egg yolk**
2 **cups unbleached flour**
½ **teaspoon baking powder**

1. In a small bowl, thoroughly mix together the boiling water and carob powder. Set aside to cool.

2. Preheat the oven to 350 degrees.

3. In a large mixing bowl, cream the butter and almond extract together. Gradually add the sugar, beating until light and fluffy. Add the egg yolk, and beat thoroughly.

4. Sir in the cooled carob mixture. Combine the flour and baking powder and add to the dough a quarter at a time, mixing well after each addition.

5. Fit a cookie press with a star-shaped nozzle and press the cookies out onto an unbuttered cookie sheet. Bake for 12 minutes. Cool on wire racks.

Makes 60 to 70 cookies.

Oat Boats

½   **cup butter, softened**
1   **egg**
1   **teaspoon pure vanilla extract**
1   **teaspoon grated orange peel**
1   **teaspoon grated lemon peel**
1   **cup chopped pitted dates**
⅓   **cup unsweetened carob powder**
1   **cup rolled oats**
½   **cup pastry flour**
½   **cup wheat germ**
1   **teaspoon baking powder**
½   **teaspoon ground allspice**
½   **teaspoon ground nutmeg**
½   **teaspoon ground cinnamon**
⅔   **cup milk**

1. Preheat the oven to 325 degrees.

2. Beat the butter and egg together until well combined. Add the vanilla, grated peels, dates, and carob powder and mix well.

3. Mix together the oats, flour, wheat germ, baking powder, allspice, nutmeg, and cinnamon. Add to the creamed mixture, alternately with the milk, beating well after each addition.

4. Spread the batter in a buttered 10- x 15- x 2-inch baking pan. Sprinkle with carob chips, nuts, or any powder from The Spice Capsule (see page 22).

5. Bake for 25 minutes. Cut into oblong bars and cool on a wire rack.

Makes about 2 dozen.

Cinnamon Chippies

½ cup unsalted butter, softened
½ cup honey or other liquid sweetener
1 egg
1 teaspoon pure vanilla extract
1¼ cups sifted whole-wheat pastry flour
1 teaspoon baking powder
2 tablespoons wheat germ
1 teaspoon ground cinnamon
1 cup carob chips
1 cup chopped nuts

1. Cream the butter. Slowly beat in the honey until the mixture is light and fluffy. Add the egg and vanilla and beat well.

2. Sift together the flour and baking powder and stir into the creamed mixture. Add the wheat germ, cinnamon, carob chips, and nuts and mix well. Chill the dough thoroughly.

3. Preheat the oven to 350 degrees.

4. Drop the dough by teaspoons onto a lightly oiled or buttered baking sheet. Bake for 12 to 15 minutes.

Makes 5 dozen cookies.

Variation: Fresh minced or crushed dried carnation petals can be substituted for the ground cinnamon.

Bench Warmers

1 **cup unsalted butter, softened**
¼ **teaspoon freshly ground black pepper**
1 **teaspoon fresh ginger juice**
½ **cup unsweetened carob powder**
1½ **cups unsulphured molasses**
   Pinch of freshly ground nutmeg
⅓ **cup hot herb tea**
2 **teaspoons baking soda**
4½ **cups sifted unbleached flour or whole-wheat pastry flour**
   Nuts or fruits for decoration

1. Put the butter, black pepper, ginger juice, carob powder, and molasses in a large bowl and beat until creamy.

2. Blend the nutmeg, herb tea, and baking soda together, and combine with the creamed mixture.

3. Gradually add in the sifted flour. Knead the dough well, wrap it in wax paper, and chill for at least 1 hour.

4. Preheat the oven to 300 degrees.

5. Roll the dough out to a ⅜-inch thickness on a floured board. Cut the dough into gingerbread men shapes and decorate with nuts or fruits. Carefully sit the gingerbread men up around the inside of a buttered deep round or square cake pan. The shoulders of the men should be touching.

6. Bake for 10 to 15 minutes.

Makes about 2½ dozen sitters.

Double-Carob Cookies

½ **cup unsalted butter, softened, or unrefined vegetable oil**

½ **cup honey**

1 **egg**

½ **cup sour cream or plain yogurt**

1 **teaspoon pure vanilla extract**

2 **cups unbleached flour**

½ **cup unsweetened carob powder**

½ **teaspoon baking soda**

½ **cup carob chips**

1. Preheat the oven to 375 degrees.

2. In a large mixing bowl, beat the butter and honey together until fluffy. Beat in the egg, sour cream, and vanilla.

3. Combine the flour, carob powder, and baking soda and beat the mixture gradually into the creamed mixture. Stir in the carob chips.

4. Drop by teaspoons onto a buttered baking sheet. Bake for 8 to 10 minutes. Cool slightly before removing to wire racks.

Makes about 4 dozen cookies.

Whole-Wheat Toll House Cookies

2   cups whole-wheat pastry flour
¼   cup unbleached flour
1   teaspoon baking soda
1   cup unsalted butter, softened
¼   cup date sugar
1   cup honey
1   teaspoon pure vanilla extract
     Pinch of ground nutmeg
1   egg
2   cups carob chips
1   cup coarsely chopped nuts

1. Preheat the oven to 375 degrees.

2. Combine the flours and baking soda together and set aside.

3. In a large mixing bowl, beat the butter, sugar, honey, vanilla, and nutmeg together until creamy. Beat in the egg.

4. Add the flour mixture and mix until completely combined. Stir in the chips and nuts.

5. Drop by rounded teaspoons onto buttered baking sheets. Bake for 8 to 10 minutes.

Makes 2 dozen cookies.

Nut-Niks

1 cup unsalted butter, softened, or unrefined vegetable oil
½ cup honey
4 tablespoons unsweetened carob powder
1 cup mashed potatoes
1 egg
1½ cups whole-wheat flour
1 teaspoon cream of tartar
1 teaspoon baking soda
2 teaspoons pure vanilla extract

1. In a large mixing bowl, cream the butter until smooth. Beat in the honey and carob powder. Add the potatoes and beat until well blended.

2. Mix together the flour, cream of tartar, and baking soda and stir into the creamed mixture until completely incorporated. Stir in the vanilla. Chill the dough for at least ½ hour.

3. Preheat the oven to 350 degrees.

4. Drop the dough by rounded teaspoons onto buttered baking sheets. Bake for 15 minutes. Cool on wire racks.

Makes 2 dozen cookies.

"Mud" Pie

Half cake, half pudding-pie, this dessert can be served with whipped cream.

  1 **cup whole-wheat pastry flour**
1½ **teaspoons baking powder**
  5 **tablespoons unsweetened carob powder**
  ½ **cup honey**
  2 **tablespoons melted unsalted butter or un-refined vegetable oil**
  ¼ **cup plain yogurt**
  1 **teaspoon pure vanilla extract**
  ½ **cup chopped nuts (optional)**
1½ **cups hot water**
    Sweetened whipped cream

1. Preheat the oven to 350 degrees.

2. Sift the flour, baking powder, and 3 tablespoons of the carob powder into a mixing bowl. Add ¼ cup honey, the melted butter, yogurt, vanilla, and nuts. Mix well.

3. Spread the batter evenly in a buttered 9-inch square baking pan. Combine the remaining ¼ cup honey and 2 tablespoons carob powder with the hot water. Mix well and pour over the batter in the pan.

4. Bake for 45 minutes. The cake will rise to the top and the carob sauce will form on the bottom. Serve warm.

Makes 4 to 6 servings.

Variation: This may be prepared as 4 individual servings. Pour the batter and sauce into 4 large buttered custard cups and bake for 35 minutes.

Quick Carob-Mint Pie

1½   **pounds tofu (bean curd)**
½   **cup light honey**
½   **cup sifted unsweetened carob powder**
 4   **teaspoons pure vanilla extract**
¼   **teaspoon pure peppermint extract, or 2 large fresh mint leaves, minced**
½   **teaspoon freshly ground cinnamon stick**
 1   **unbaked 9-inch pie shell**
      Toasted nuts or shredded coconut for garnish

1. Preheat the oven to 425 degrees.

2. Put the tofu, honey, carob powder, vanilla and peppermint extracts, and ground cinnamon in the container of a blender and blend until very smooth. (You may have to do this in two batches.)

3. Pour into the pie shell and bake for 15 minutes. Cool and garnish as desired.

Makes 6 servings.

Variation: For a low-calorie version, bake the blended custard in greased custard cups and serve as a pudding with or without a sauce.

Cocoa Crust

1 **cup whole-grain flour**
⅓ **cup ground nuts**
¼ **cup unsweetened carob powder**
½ **cup unsalted butter or unrefined vegetable oil**
½ **teaspoon pure vanilla extract, or 1 teaspoon herbal tea leaves of your choice**
2 **to 3 tablespoons cold water**

1. Preheat the oven to 400 degrees

2. In a medium-sized bowl, combine the flour, ground nuts, and carob powder. Cut in the butter with a pastry blender or 2 knives, until the mixture resembles coarse meal.

3. Add the vanilla and enough water to form the dough into a ball.

4. Roll the dough out to a ⅛-inch thickness on a lightly floured board. Fit the dough into a 9-inch pie pan and prick all over with a fork. Trim the dough and crimp the edges around the pie plate.

5. Bake for 8 minutes. The crust will be soft and bubbly when you take it from the oven, but will become firm as it cools.

Makes 1 9-inch pie crust.

Variation: For a Cocoa-Coco Crust, substitute ⅓ cup flaked coconut for the ground nuts.

Coconut Nests

These little shells make great holders for cold puddings, custards, and ice cream.

4 ounces block carob, broken into pieces
2 tablespoons unsalted butter
2 cups unsweetened flaked coconut
Pinch of ground mace

1. Draw five 3-inch circles on a sheet of wax paper. Put the wax paper on a baking sheet and set it aside.

2. Put the carob and butter into a small heavy saucepan. Heat over low heat, stirring constantly, until the carob melts. Remove from the heat and stir in the coconut and mace.

3. Put about ⅓ cup of the mixture on each circle on the wax paper and spread to cover the circle. With the back of a small spoon, push the coconut mixture from the center to form sides. Refrigerate until firm.

Makes 5 servings.

Toppings

Spiderwebs

1. Melt chunks of carob or carob chips in the top of a double boiler over hot, not boiling, water.

2. When the carob has cooled but not set, spoon it into a pastry bag fitted with a plain tip.

3. Pipe the carob through the tube to make five to six circles around the top of the cake.

4. Pull the dull edge of a table knife across the circles from the center to the outer edge. Repeat eight or ten times.

Decorative Cutouts

1. Line a baking sheet with foil.

2. Melt chunks of carob or carob chips in the top of a double boiler over hot, not boiling, water. Pour the melted carob onto the prepared baking sheet. Cool until almost set.

3. Cut the carob sheet into designs, using a cookie cutter for large shapes, or canapé cutters for small shapes. Do not remove the shapes from the baking sheet.

4. Chill the baking sheet until the carob is firm. Use a spatula to remove each of the cutouts from the foil. Use the cutouts to decorate frosted or glazed cakes.

Carob Leaves

1. Wash an assortment of leaves from non-poisonous plants (such as roses or geraniums). Pat the leaves dry with paper towels.

2. Melt chunks of carob or carob chips in the top of a double boiler over hot, not boiling, water.

3. Use a narrow spatula or knife to spread a layer of melted chocolate ⅛ inch thick on the *back* of each leaf. Spread the carob just to the edge; don't let any chocolate spill over to the front of the leaf.

4. Lay the leaves, carob side up, on a flat pan or tray. Chill until firm.

5. Carefully peel off the leaves and use the carob leaves to decorate cakes or other desserts.

Allegretti Decoration

1. Frost your cake with your favorite white frosting. Swirl the sides and top of the cake with a spatula. Let the cake stand until the frosting is firm.

2. Melt chunks of carob with ½ teaspoon unsalted butter in the top of a double boiler over hot, not boiling, water. Cool slightly.

3. Drop the melted carob mixture from the tip of a teaspoon around the top edge of the frosted cake, so that it dribbles down the sides of the cake.

Citrus Dribble

¾ **cup honey**
2 **tablespoons coarsely shredded orange peel**
⅓ **cup warm water or citrus herb tea**

Mix all ingredients together thoroughly. Dribble evenly over cake layers or cupcakes. Let the syrup soak into the cakes before serving.

Makes 1¼ cups.

Sugar-Free Cookie Icing

1 **egg white**
¼ **cup honey or unsweetened carob syrup**
½ **teaspoon pure peppermint extract or any other pure extract of your choice**

1. Beat the egg white until it holds soft peaks.

2. While still beating, slowly add the honey and peppermint extract. Beat until the icing is stiff and glossy.

Makes 1 cup.

Milk-Free Frosting

This is a great substitute for whipped cream.

⅔ **cup soy milk powder**
1 **cup lukewarm water**
2 **tablespoons unrefined vegetable oil**
   Honey
   Lemon juice
   1. Put the milk powder, water, and oil into the container of a blender. Add honey and lemon juice to taste. Blend until smooth and creamy.
   2. Continue adding lemon juice, drop by drop, blending until the mixture is thick. Chill thoroughly before using.

Makes about 1½ cups.

Date Icing

This sugar-free icing is a good topping for cupcakes.

¼ **cup water**
½ **cup chopped pitted dates**
¼ **cup nut or unrefined vegetable oil**
   1. Put the water and dates into the container of an electric blender. Blend until smooth.
   2. With the blender still running, add the oil a little at a time, until the icing is creamy and smooth.

Makes 1 cup.

Variation: Dust the iced cupcakes with carob "sprinkles" (see page 23).

Carob–Sour Cream Icing

This is good on cupcakes or cake layers.

5 **ounces carob chips**
½ **cup sour cream or plain yogurt**

   1. Melt the carob chips in the top of a double boiler over hot water. Cool.

   2. Beat the sour cream into the cooled carob until well blended.

Makes 1 cup.

Hot Carob Dribble

Use this icing warm and dribble it over cooled cupcakes and cake layers.

1 **cup carob chips**
2 **tablespoons unsalted butter**
2 **tablespoons honey**
3 **tablespoons heavy cream**

   1. Combine the chips and butter in the top of a double boiler over hot, not boiling, water. Stir until melted and well combined.

   2. Remove the top of the double boiler from the heat and stir in the honey and cream. Beat until smooth. Use the icing while it is warm.

Makes 1 cup.

Cold Carob Dribble

This can be used to drizzle over warm cakes and desserts or it can be eaten as a pudding.

⅓ **cup sour cream**
⅓ **cup soft tofu (bean curd)**
½ **cup plain yogurt**
2 **teaspoons unsweetened carob powder, or to taste**

Put all the ingredients into the container of a blender. Blend until smooth. If the icing is too thick, thin it with more cream.

Makes 1 cup.

Carob-Cherry Icing

8 **tablespoons unsweetened carob powder**
4 **tablespoons arrowroot or cornstarch**
6 **tablespoons honey**
¼ **cup heavy cream**
2 **tablespoons cherry concentrate**
¼ **cup chopped pitted dried cherries (optional)**

1. Combine the carob powder and arrowroot. Beat in the honey gradually, beating well after each addition.

2. Stir in the cream a little at a time, blending

well after each addition. Add the cherry concentrate and stir until the icing reaches spreading consistency. Stir in the chopped cherries and mix well.

Makes 1½ cups.

Variations: Any pure fruit concentrate can be substituted for the cherry concentrate.

Chopped raisins can be substituted for the chopped cherries.

Doublemint Dribble

This makes a good glaze for cupcakes and cake layers.

1   egg white
¼   cup honey
½   teaspoon double-strength peppermint tea
½   teaspoon double-strength spearmint tea

Beat the egg white until stiff. Using a wire whisk, gradually beat in the honey and the peppermint and spearmint tea. Beat until the icing thickens. (If the icing doesn't thicken after a while, you can add a small amount of dry milk powder, beating it in well.)

Makes 1 cup.

Honey Icing

1 **teaspoon unflavored gelatin**
¼ **cup cold water**
¼ **cup honey or maple syrup**
½ **cup warm water**
1 **cup dry milk powder, sifted**

1. In a small bowl, sprinkle the gelatin over the cold water. Let sit for 5 minutes to soften.

2. Put the honey and warm water into a small saucepan and bring to a boil. Remove from the heat and stir in the softened gelatin, stirring until the gelatin is dissolved. Gradually add the sifted dry milk powder, blending until the glaze is smooth. Use while warm.

Makes 1 cup.

Bubblin' Brown Sugar Frosting

This is delicious on homemade doughnuts.

⅓ **cup unsalted butter**
¼ **cup date sugar**
¼ **cup water**
¾ **cup dry milk powder**
1 **teaspoon pure vanilla extract**

1. Melt the butter in a small heavy saucepan, and let it cook until it just starts to turn brown.

2. Add the sugar, water, dry milk powder, and vanilla. Combine well and cook, stirring, over low heat for 3 to 5 minutes, or until smooth.

Makes 1½ cups.

Lemon Glaze

This glaze stays moist and sticky—and it's so good to lick off your fingers.

¼ cup honey
¼ cup fresh lemon or lime juice
¼ cup dry milk powder

Put all the ingredients in a small heavy saucepan and mix to combine well. Bring to a boil and boil for 3 minutes, stirring occasionally. Cool for 1 minute before drizzling over cake layers or cupcakes.

Makes ½ cup.

Whipped "Fudge" Topping

This is delicious spread on carob brownies or as a garnish for carob cocoa.

2 tablespoons cold water
2 teaspoons unflavored gelatin
½ cup boiling water
⅓ cup dry milk powder
2 tablespoons unsweetened carob powder
½ teaspoon pure vanilla extract
4 to 6 ice cubes

1. Put the cold water into the container of a blender. Sprinkle the gelatin over the water and let it soften for 5 minutes.

2. Add the boiling water and blend until the gelatin is dissolved.

3. With the blender on low, gradually add the dry milk powder, carob powder, and vanilla, blending until smooth.

4. With the blender still running, add the ice cubes one at a time, blending until the mixture thickens.

Makes 1½ cups.

"Mud"

This very fudgy sauce is a great topping for plain cake.

6 **heaping tablespoons unsweetened carob powder**
½ **cup water**
1 **vanilla bean, split lengthwise**
2 **tablespoons soy flour**
½ **cup currants, chopped raisins, chopped dates, or chopped cherries**
1 **heaping tablespoon arrowroot or cornstarch**
2 **tablespoons nut butter**

1. Put the carob and the water in a small saucepan. Stir to dissolve the carob. Bring to a boil and add the split vanilla bean. Cover the pan, lower the heat, and simmer for 15 minutes.

2. Remove the pan from the heat and remove the vanilla bean. Use a wire whisk to beat the soy flour into the syrup.

3. Add the currants to the syrup, bring back to a boil, cover, lower the heat, and simmer for 15 minutes.

4. Dissolve the arrowroot in a small amount of the syrup and add the arrowroot to the syrup in the saucepan. Stir over low heat until the syrup is thick. Remove from the heat. Cool the syrup slightly.

5. Pour into the container of a blender and blend until smooth.

Makes about 3 cups.

Variations: For a Double-"Mud" Frosting, add 2 to 4 tablespoons sesame butter or almond butter and 2 more tablespoons sweetened carob powder to the blended mixture above. Blend until smooth.

Add a bit of "Mud" to muffin or cookie batters to "chocolafy" them.

Crackers, Breads, Rolls, Muffins

Saint John's Crisps

The mixture of carob and caraway gives these crackers a pumpernickel tang.

- **1 tablespoon active dry yeast**
- **½ cup lukewarm water**
- **1 cup rye flour**
- **3 tablespoons unsweetened carob powder**
- **½ teaspoon ascorbate powder of kelp (optional)**
- **1 teaspoon caraway seeds**

1. Sprinkle the yeast over the water. Set aside for 5 minutes.

2. Combine the flour, carob powder, ascorbate powder, and caraway seeds in a medium-sized bowl.

3. When the yeast is bubbly, stir it into the dry ingredients, mixing until the dough forms a ball which comes away from the sides of the bowl.

4. Butter a baking sheet well. Put the dough in the middle of the baking sheet and pat it out to a thickness of ⅛ inch. (The dough should not be any thinner, or it will be difficult to remove from the sheet; any thicker and it won't get crisp.)

5. Use a sharp knife to score the dough in a square or diamond pattern. Cover with a damp towel and let rise in a warm, draft-free place for 45 minutes.

6. Put the baking sheet into a cold oven. Turn the oven temperature to 225 degrees and bake for 15 minutes. Raise the oven temperature to 300 degrees and bake for 15 to 20 minutes, or until brown. Let the crackers cool on the sheet for 5 minutes before removing and separating them.

Makes about 2 dozen crackers.

Note: This dough also makes a good pie crust. You will not have to let it rise. Just pat it out or roll it to fit your pie pan, prick it well with a fork, and proceed as you would with a regular pie shell.

Wrinkled Fruit Bread

12 ounces dried apples
12 ounces dried prunes
12 ounces dried dates
1 cup apple cider
2 packages active dry yeast
2 cups warm (about 110 degrees) water
¼ cup honey
¼ cup homemade fruit sugar
1 teaspoon ascorbate powder or kelp
1 tablespoon aniseed
1 teaspoon ground cinnamon
½ teaspoon ground cloves
½ teaspoon ground cardamom
½ cup wheat germ
½ cup melted unsalted butter
6 cups, approximately, unsifted unbleached or whole-wheat flour
1 cup sifted unsweetened carob powder
1 cup dates, coarsely chopped
½ cup coarsely chopped unblanched almonds
½ cup coarsely chopped walnuts
Melted unsalted butter

1. Cut the apples, prunes, and dates into ½-inch pieces. Put the fruits in a saucepan with the cider and heat until the liquid is just hot. Remove from the heat and set aside. Stir occasionally while the mixture cools.

2. Put the yeast and ½ cup warm water into a large mixing bowl and let sit for 5 minutes. Stir in the remaining water, honey, sugar, ascorbate powder, aniseed, cinnamon, cloves, cardamom, wheat germ, and melted butter. Gradually add 3½ cups of the flour while beating at medium speed. Beat for 5 minutes.

3. Gradually mix in 2 more cups of the flour using a wooden spoon or dough hook.

4. Turn the dough out onto a board that has been sprinkled with the remaining ½ cup flour and the carob powder. Knead until the dough is smooth and no longer sticky, about 5 to 10 minutes. Add more flour to the board if necessary.

5. Put the dough in a greased bowl and turn to grease the top. Cover the bowl with a damp towel and let the dough rise in a warm place for about 1½ hours, or until doubled.

6. Stir the chopped dates and nuts into the soaked fruits.

7. Turn the dough out on a lightly floured board and knead gently again. Flatten the dough to a circle about ½ inch thick. Put about half the fruit mixture on top of the dough and knead it in gently, pulling the dough over the fruit as you work it through the dough. Add only enough flour as needed to keep the dough from sticking. Flatten the dough again and knead in the remaining fruit.

8. Divide the dough in half and shape each half into a loaf. Put the dough in well-buttered 9- x 5-inch loaf pans. Cover lightly and let rise in a warm place for about 1 hour, or until doubled.

9. Preheat the oven to 350 degrees.

10. Brush the loaves lightly with the melted butter. Bake for about 1 hour, or until the bread starts to pull away from the sides of the pans. (If the tops of the loaves begin to brown too much, cover them lightly with foil.) Remove the loaves from the pans and cool thoroughly on wire racks before wrapping in foil or plastic.

Makes 2 loaves.

Magic Muffins

To perform this magic act, the wheat must be hot and freshly cooked.

4 cups hot cooked cracked wheat or short-grain brown rice
½ cup carob chips or curls
2 cups fresh sliced strawberries, or an equal amount of soaked, drained and slivered dried fruit

1. Alternate layers of the three ingredients in buttered cast-iron popover tins or muffin tins. Press down firmly to compact the ingredients.

2. Chill until cool. Use a table knife to loosen the muffins from the tins. Butter and serve.

Makes 8 to 10 muffins.

Instant Cinnamon Rolls

1 handful bread dough
Melted unsalted butter
Ground cinnamon
Unsweetened carob powder
Raw bran or crushed seeds

1. Roll the dough out and dribble on some melted butter. Sprinkle some cinnamon, carob powder, and raw bran over the melted butter.

2. Roll the dough up like a jelly-roll. Cover with a damp towel and let rise in a warm place until doubled.

3. Preheat the oven to 350 degrees.

4. Slice the cinnamon roll in ½-inch-thick slices and put the slices on a buttered baking sheet. Bake for 20 minutes.

Makes 12 rolls.

Carobana Bread

4 **cups whole-wheat or whole-grain flour**
½ **cup unsweetened carob powder**
1½ **teaspoons baking powder**
1 **tablespoon ground allspice**
½ **cup natural liquid sweetener**
½ **teaspoon pure vanilla extract**
2 **ripe bananas**
¾ **to 1 cup water**

1. Preheat the oven to 350 degrees. Butter an 8- or 9-inch square baking pan, and dust it liberally with carob powder.

2. Combine the flour, carob powder, baking powder, and allspice in a large bowl.

3. Put the sweetener, vanilla, bananas, and water into the container of a blender and blend until smooth. (You should have approximately 2½ cups of purée.)

4. Stir the purée into the flour mixture and combine well. Pour the batter into the prepared pan and bake for 35 minutes, or until a toothpick inserted in the center comes out clean. Cool in the pan and cut into squares.

Makes 12 servings.

Variation: One-half cup raisins or chopped nuts may be added to the batter before it is poured into the pan.

Carob-Bran Bagels

1   **cup bran**
⅓ **cup honey**
⅓ **cup dark molasses or unsweetened carob syrup**
3   **tablespoons unsweetened carob powder**
2   **cups boiling water**
2   **packages active dry yeast**
2   **cups rye flour**
2   **cups unbleached flour**
1   **cup whole-wheat flour**

1. Put the bran in a dry frying pan and toast it over a very low flame until it is brown. Set aside.

2. Dissolve the honey, molasses, and carob powder in the boiling water. Let the mixture cool to 110 to 115 degrees. Then add the yeast and let it dissolve. Stir the flours and bran into the yeast mixture until a dough is formed.

3. Put the dough on a floured surface and spread flour over the dough. Flour your hands and knead the dough for about 10 minutes.

4. Put the dough in a buttered bowl and turn the dough to grease the top. Cover the bowl with a damp towel and let the dough rise for about 1 hour, or until doubled.

5. Punch the dough down and divide it into 24 equal portions. Dust your hands with flour and roll each piece of dough into a rope 6 to 7 inches long. Pinch the ends together to seal.

6. As you complete the bagels, put them on a floured board. Cover with a damp towel and let rise in a warm place for about 20 minutes.

7. Bring 2 quarts of water to a boil. Drop 3 or 4 bagels at a time into the boiling water. When they rise to the surface, turn them. Cook for 2 minutes and remove to paper towels with a slotted spoon. Let drain.

8. Preheat the oven to 425 degrees.

9. Sprinkle baking sheets with cornmeal and set the drained bagels on the cornmeal. Bake for 20 to 30 minutes, or until brown and firm. (You may want to rotate the bagels, or turn them halfway during baking, if your oven heats unevenly.)

Makes 24 bagels.

Puddings, Frozen Desserts

Unyogurt

This is delicious spread on homemade crackers, sourdough bread, or as a dip for raw vegetables.

¼ **cup flax seeds**
¼ **cup shredded coconut**
¼ **cup unsweetened carob powder**
¼ **cup rolled oats**
¼ **cup sunflower seeds**

Combine all the ingredients in a large bowl. Cover with fresh water and stir to mix well. Cover the bowl tightly and let the mixture ferment for 2 days in a warm place. The consistency will be very much like yogurt.

Makes 2 cups.

Powder Puffs

2   **envelopes unflavored gelatin**
½   **cup boiling water**
1½ **cups dry milk powder**
1   **cup cold water**
6   **tablespoons unsweetened carob powder**
¼   **cup honey**
2   **teaspoons pure vanilla extract**
9   **ice cubes (about 2 cups)**

    1. Put the gelatin and boiling water in the container of a blender, cover, and blend at medium speed for 60 seconds.

    2. Add the dry milk powder and cold water and blend briefly. Add the carob powder, honey, and vanilla and blend until smooth.

    3. Add the ice cubes and blend at high speed just until the ice is pulverized. Uncover the blender and let the mixture stand for about 5 minutes to set. Serve immediately.

    Makes 4 servings.

Chia Seed "Chocolate" Pudding

⅔ cup dry sunflower seeds
4 cups water
8 teaspoons chia seeds
4 cups whole, soy, or seed milk
4 tablespoons unsweetened carob powder
Honey or other natural sweetener to taste

Put the sunflower seeds in the container of a blender. Blend while slowly adding the water. Add the chia seeds and blend until smooth. Add the remaining ingredients and blend again.

Makes 8 servings.

Mock Chocolate Mousse

2 unsprayed, unwaxed yellow Delicious apples
Apple juice
1 teaspoon lemon juice
1 teaspoon soy lecithin granules
1 cup ground raw cashews
2 tablespoons sifted unsweetened carob powder
Slivered almonds

1. Core and cube, but do not peel, the apples. Put them in the container of a blender with just enough apple juice to purée them. Blend in the lemon juice and soy lecithin granules.

2. Gradually add the ground raw cashews to the apple purée, blending until the mixture is smooth. Stir in the carob powder and pour the custard into small cups. Chill. Sprinkle with the almonds before serving.

Makes 4 servings.

Mighty Mousse

This super dessert is cocoa-free, but very chocolatey.

1   **pound ricotta cheese**
1   **tablespoon unsweetened carob powder**
1   **teaspoon decaffeinated coffee powder or herbal coffee powder**
¼   **cup dry milk powder**
2   **tablespoons honey**
1   **tablespoon almond oil**
    Fresh violets or rosebuds for garnish

Put all the ingredients in the container of a blender or food processor and blend until smooth. Refrigerate for 1 hour before serving. Garnish with the fresh flowers.

Makes 6 servings.

Variation: For a less sweet, low-cholesterol, and low-calorie version, substitute mashed soft tofu (bean curd) or plain yogurt for the ricotta.

Carob Ripple

10 **ripe medium-sized bananas**
½ **pound dried figs, cut up**
 Water
1 **cup unsweetened carob powder**

1. Peel the bananas, cut them into chunks, and put the chunks in the container of a blender. Blend until they form a creamy purée. Pour the purée into an ice cube tray and freeze until it is just beginning to harden.

2. Put the figs in the container of a blender and add just enough water to blend the figs into a thin paste. Add the carob powder and blend thoroughly.

3. Remove the banana purée from the freezer and swirl the fig mixture into the center of the partially frozen purée. Return to the freezer to harden completely before serving.

Makes 8 servings.

Carob Ice Cream Cones

Any broken cones can be eaten as cookies or stuck into dished-up ice cream as edible decorations.

¼ **cup dry milk powder**
¼ **cup unsweetened carob powder**
½ **cup pastry flour, sifted**
2 **egg whites, beaten stiffly**
2 **egg yolks, beaten**
4 **tablespoons water or milk**
¼ **cup unrefined vegetable oil**
1 **teaspoon pure vanilla extract**

1. Combine the dry milk powder, carob powder, and flour and set aside.

2. Fold the beaten egg whites into the egg yolks until completely combined. Then gently stir in the water, oil, and vanilla. Beat in the dry ingredients until the batter is very smooth.

3. Heat a heavy skillet, griddle, or Krumkake iron until very hot. Butter well and spread on it 1 teaspoon of the batter as thinly as possible. Let brown and turn to briefly brown the other side.

4. Remove the cookie from the pan and immediately shape it around a cone form which has been made from lightweight cardboard. When cool, set the ice cream cone aside and continue making cones until all the batter is used.

Makes about 3 dozen cones.

Carob Granita

½ **cup water**
¼ **cup honey**
¼ **cup homemade sugar**
1 **tablespoon grated orange peel**
¼ **cup strong carob cocoa**
2 **ounces block carob**

1. In a saucepan, combine the water, honey, sugar, and orange peel. Bring to a boil over moderate heat, stirring until the sugar has dissolved. Lower the heat and simmer the syrup for 5 minutes. Stir in the carob cocoa and let the syrup cool to lukewarm.

2. Melt the block carob in the top of a double boiler over hot, not boiling, water. Remove the double boiler top from over the water and let the carob cool to lukewarm.

3. Add the cooled syrup to the melted carob in a slow stream, beating constantly. Pour into an ice cube tray and freeze until firm but not hard.

4. Transfer the granita to the container of a food processor or to a bowl and beat until it is smooth. Return the granita to the ice cube tray and freeze for 3 hours, or until it is hard. Let the granita stand at room temperature for 5 minutes before serving.

Makes 4 servings.

Lickety Splits

1. Cut fresh papaya, persimmons, mangos, and/or kiwi fruit into quarters and arrange in individual dessert dishes.

2. Put a scoop of vanilla ice cream on top of the fruit and drizzle honey or maple syrup over the ice cream. Sprinkle some carob chips or curls on top of the honey, and add some chopped nuts.

3. Top the splits with one of the following "whipped" creams:

> Ricotta cheese puréed with a dash of pure vanilla extract, *or*
>
> Puréed fresh tofu, blended with 1 teaspoon of honey, *or*
>
> Puréed cottage cheese, blended with homemade sugar or bee pollen.

Creamy Carob Pops

3 ounces ricotta or farmer cheese, or **4** ounces tofu
⅓ cup maple syrup
2 teaspoons pure vanilla extract
½ teaspoon ground cinnamon
¼ teaspoon ground ginger
2 tablespoons unsweetened carob powder
¾ to 1 cup water

Beat all ingredients together until well blended. Pour into popsicle molds or paper cups and freeze until partially frozen. Insert popsicle sticks into the center of each mold and freeze solid.

Makes 8 pops.

Variation: For crunchy pops, stir in ½ cup toasted oats, carob grits, or unsweetened flaked coconut before freezing.

Carob Rocky Road

10 ripe bananas
⅓ cup sweetened carob powder
1½ cups chopped dried apricots

1. Peel the bananas and cut them into chunks. Put the chunks into the container of a blender and blend until they form a creamy purée. Add the carob and blend until well combined. Pour the mixture into 2 ice cube trays and freeze until firm but not hard.

2. Transfer the ice cream to a bowl and beat until smooth. Stir in the apricots.

3. Return the ice cream to the trays and freeze for 3 hours, or until it is hard.

Makes 6 to 8 servings.

Variation: For Rocky Road pops, pour the fruited ice cream into popsicle molds or paper cups and freeze until a popsicle stick can be inserted in the center of each mold. Then freeze until solid.

The Ultimate Ice Cream Sandwich

8 **½- to ¾-inch thick slices brick-style ice cream**
32 **sugar-free graham crackers**
18 **ounces block carob or carob chips**
4 **tablespoons unsalted butter**

1. Cut each ice cream slice in half and put the slices between two graham crackers. Put the "sandwiches" on a baking sheet and freeze until firm.

2. Melt the carob in the top of a double boiler over hot, not boiling, water. Add the butter and stir until the butter has melted and the melted carob is smooth. Do not *overheat*.

3. Remove the sandwiches from the freezer and coat the edges of each sandwich with the melted carob, using a pastry brush. Then coat the top of each sandwich with the melted carob. Freeze, uncovered, for 45 minutes.

4. Gently reheat the carob and when it is spreadable, turn the sandwiches and coat the other side. Freeze again until firm. Wrap in foil and store in the freezer.

Makes 16 ice cream sandwiches.

Variations: Popsicle sticks can be pushed into the ice cream to make Eskimo-type pies.

For crunch bars, sprinkle the melted carob with toasted buttered flaked almonds before freezing.

Banana-Carob Cream

5 **pitted dates**
½ **cup raw cashews**
2 **tablespoons unsweetened carob powder**
¾ **cup water**
1 **teaspoon pure vanilla extract**
4 **to 5 ripe bananas**

1. Put the dates, cashews, carob powder, water, and vanilla into the container of a blender and purée.

2. Peel the bananas and cut them into chunks. With the blender running, add the banana chunks slowly until a thick purée is formed.

3. Pour the mixture into an ice cube tray and freeze until hard. (Or, serve immediately as a soft ice cream.)

Makes 4 to 6 servings.

Variation: For Banana-Carob Chip Cream, add 4 ounces chopped regular or mint carob to the thickened purée.

Pepsicles

6 large ripe bananas
Sweetened carob syrup or sauce
Toasted nuts, toasted sprouts, toasted oat flakes, unsweetened flaked coconut, grated citrus peel, or finely diced dried fruit

1. Peel the bananas and put them on a baking sheet. Put in the freezer until the bananas are almost hard.

2. Remove the bananas from the freezer and cut them in half. Insert popsicle sticks in the cut ends of each banana. Roll the banana halves in carob syrup and then in the toasted nuts. After each banana half is coated, lay it on the baking sheet, making sure the halves don't touch. Return to the freezer until hard.

Makes 12 pops.

Variation: The banana halves can be rolled in honey or maple syrup and sprinkled with carob curls.

Sauces, Marinades

Carob Sauce I

This makes a rich dessert sauce.

¼ **cup unsweetened carob powder**
¼ **cup honey**
⅔ **cup milk**
½ **teaspoon pure vanilla extract**

Combine all the ingredients in a small heavy saucepan. Bring to a boil while stirring with a wire whisk or wooden spoon. Lower the heat and simmer for 5 minutes, stirring occasionally. Cool and store in a screw-top jar in the refrigerator.

Makes 1 cup.

Carob Sauce II

This is a very rich dessert sauce.

2 **tablespoons unsalted butter**
⅓ **cup honey**
⅓ **cup water**
⅓ **cup unsweetened carob powder**
1 **egg**
1 **teaspoon pure vanilla extract**

Combine all the ingredients in a small heavy saucepan. Cook over low heat, stirring with a wire whisk or wooden spoon, until the sauce is thick and smooth. Cool and store in a screw-top jar in the refrigerator.

Makes 2 cups.

Carob Sauce III

This makes the richest of the dessert sauces—and it's very, very good.

2 **tablespoons unsweetened carob powder**
1 **tablespoon boiling water**
1 **large egg yolk**
¼ **cup thick honey**
¼ **cup heavy cream, whipped stiff**

1. Dissolve the carob powder in the boiling water. Set aside to cool slightly.

2. Beat the egg yolk until light. Beat in the honey and then beat in the carob mixture. Fold in the whipped cream and stir until very smooth.

Makes 1½ cups.

"Soft" Sauce

If you don't care for hard sauce, try spooning this over warm or cold cake—or the next plum pudding you make.

3 **ounces block carob**
¼ **cup water**
¼ **cup honey or maple syrup**
Pinch of ground cinnamon
½ **teaspoon pure vanilla extract**
½ **cup heavy cream**

1. Melt the carob in the top of a double boiler over hot, not boiling, water. Stir the carob as it melts so it does not burn. Set aside.

2. Combine the water and honey in a small saucepan and bring to a boil. Boil, stirring, for 5 minutes. Remove from the heat and cool to room temperature.

3. Stir the syrup into the melted carob and blend thoroughly. Add the cinnamon, vanilla, and cream, stirring until the sauce is smooth. Serve warm or cold.

Makes 1½ cups.

Note: To reheat, put the container of sauce in a pan of hot water for several minutes. If the sauce is too thick, thin it with a little cream.

Sour cream, crème fraîche, or thick plain yogurt may be substituted for the heavy cream to reduce the calories in the recipe.

Uncooked Carob Sauce

2   teaspoons unsweetened carob powder
3   tablespoons honey
½   cup soy milk powder
½   cup warm water

Mix the carob and honey together. Gradually add to the milk powder, alternating with the water. Stir with a wire whisk until smooth.

Makes 1½ cups.

Variation: Add 1 tablespoon lightly toasted poppy, chia, or sesame seeds for a crunchy sauce.

Carob-Nut Sauce

Serve this sauce over ice cream or frozen yogurt.

1 **tablespoon unsweetened carob powder**
2 **tablespoons boiling water**
1 **cup honey**
¼ **cup toasted slivered almonds**

Dissolve the carob powder in the boiling water. Stir in the honey and almonds and mix well.

Makes 1½ cups.

Bittersweet "Butterscotch" Sauce

Spoon this sauce over sundaes, sherbets, or stewed fruits.

16 **large pitted prunes, cut up**
½ **cup unsweetened carob syrup, or ¼ cup date sugar and**
¼ **cup unsweetened carob syrup or honey**

Put the prunes and carob syrup in the container of a blender and blend until smooth.

Makes 1 cup.

Carob-Mint Sauce

1   **cup apple juice**
2   **tablespoons pure spearmint extract**
2   **tablespoons unsweetened carob powder**
1   **tablespoon honey**
1   **very ripe banana; mashed**

    1. Heat the apple juice, spearmint, carob powder, and honey together in a saucepan for about 10 minutes, stirring until well combined.

    2. Strain the sauce and beat in the mashed banana.

Makes 1½ cups.

Variation: Stir in ½ cup coarsely crushed peanuts for a crunchy sauce.

Sweet and Sour Raisin Sauce

Serve with sliced meats or on open-faced sandwiches.

1   **cup unsulphured raisins or currants**
1   **cup water or mild herb tea**
2   **tablespoons unsweetened carob powder**
2   **tablespoons arrowroot or cornstarch**
¼   **teaspoon ground cinnamon**
¼   **teaspoon dry mustard**
¼   **teaspoon ground cloves**
1   **tablespoon vinegar**

    1. Put the raisins and water into a saucepan and bring to a boil. Boil for 5 minutes. Add the carob powder, arrowroot, cinnamon, mustard, and cloves and stir to blend. Cook over low heat until thickened, stirring with a wire whisk to prevent lumping and scorching.

2. Remove from the heat and stir in the vinegar. Blend well. The sauce may be thinned with additional water or tea, if necessary.

Makes 2½ cups.

Quick Carob Tahini

Try this dressing the next time you make tossed salad.

Blend toasted sesame seeds with a little water in the container of a blender. Gradually add sifted unsweetened carob powder until the sauce is the desired consistency.

Honey Locust Marinade

Good for chicken or other light meats.

1 cup cooked diced fresh or dried apricots
½ cup unsweetened carob syrup
1½ tablespoons unrefined vegetable oil
2 teaspoons miso (soybean paste)
1 cup orange marmalade (made with honey)
Pinch of kelp
2 tablespoons dry sherry
2 tablespoons apple cider vinegar

Put all the ingredients in a saucepan and stir well to combine. Bring to a boil, lower the heat, and simmer for 5 minutes. Cool before using.

Makes 3 cups.

Quick Carob Marinade

This is a good marinade for vegetables or slices of vegetable protein.

1 cup strong carob cocoa
½ cup unsulphured molasses
½ cup red wine vinegar
¼ cup Dijon mustard
1 tablespoon soy sauce
⅛ teaspoon cayenne pepper

Combine all the ingredients in a stainless steel or enamel saucepan. Bring to a boil over moderate heat, stirring constantly. Lower the heat and simmer for 2 minutes. Let the marinade cool and transfer it to a shallow ceramic or glass dish before using.

Makes 2 cups.

Snacks, Confections

Plain Marbles

---

24 **pitted dates, chopped**
 4 **teaspoons unsweetened carob powder**
   Honey
 ¾ **cup pecans, or other raw nuts, ground, or 1 cup sprinkles (see page 23)**

1. Purée the dates in the container of a blender. Pour into a bowl and add the carob powder. Blend with a fork, adding enough honey to make the mixture hold together. Add the ground nuts and mix them in well.

2. Break off small pieces of the mixture and roll into tiny balls. Chill before serving.

Makes 1½ dozen.

Marbleized Marbles

1 cup unsalted, hydrogenated cashew or almond butter
4 tablespoons mild honey
   Dry milk powder, whey powder, or powdered slippery elm
½ recipe for Plain Marbles

1. Blend the cashew butter with the honey until well combined. Knead in enough dry milk powder to make a stiff dough. Break off small pieces of the mixture and roll into tiny balls.

2. Shape the Plain Marble mixture into tiny balls. Press one of each kind of ball together to form marbleized marbles. Chill before serving.

Makes 2 dozen.

Crinkle Cups

These fluted carob cups make tasty holders for cold puddings, custards, and ice cream.

8 ounces block carob

1. Put 8 to 10 cupcake liners into a muffin tin. Set aside.

2. Put the carob in the top of a double boiler over hot, not boiling, water. Melt the carob partially, then take the top of the double boiler from over the hot water and stir the carob until it is completely melted. (This will keep the carob glossy.)

3. Use a pastry brush or small spoon to line the inside of the cupcake liners with the melted carob, making sure you coat all the folds evenly. (If the carob hardens, soften it again over hot water.)

4. Refrigerate the cupcake liners until serving time. When ready to use, quickly peel the paper off the cups and spoon in the filling of your choice. Serve immediately.

Makes 8 to 10 servings.

After-Dinner Mints

1 tablespoon unsalted butter
½ cup milk
1 cup mild-flavored honey
4 heaping tablespoons unsweetened carob powder
½ teaspoon pure peppermint or spearmint extract
½ cup dry milk powder

1. Melt the butter in a small heavy saucepan and add the milk, honey, and carob powder. Cook over low heat, stirring constantly, until the mixture boils. Stir at a high simmer for 3 minutes. Remove from the heat and beat until creamy.

2. Stir in the peppermint extract, then gradually add the dry milk powder, stirring until completely incorporated.

3. Spread the candy in an even thin layer over the bottom of a well-greased jelly-roll pan. Chill well. Use a biscuit cutter or a sharp knife to cut the candy into small circles or small squares or diamond shapes.

Makes 50 mints.

Dried Sprout Candy

If desired, these candies can be rolled in chopped nuts, coconut, sesame or sunflower seeds, or carob sprinkles.

4 cups dried alfalfa, wheat, or rye sprouts (see *Note*)

¼ cup brewer's yeast

½ cup dry milk powder

¼ cup unsweetened carob powder

1 cup peanut butter

1 cup chopped dried fruit

¼ to ½ cup sweetened carob syrup or honey

1. Put the sprouts in the container of a blender and blend until chopped, or chop by hand with a very sharp knife.

2. Combine the chopped sprouts with the remaining ingredients and mix well. Shape into balls, patties, or boat shapes. Chill before serving.

Makes 48 pieces.

Note: Sprouts can be oven dried by spreading them on a baking sheet in a 150-degree oven. Bake for 2 or more hours, or until the sprouts are crushable but not browned. The sprouts should have the texture of dry cereal.

Rockettes

You will enjoy this toffee-like candy.

¾ **cup light honey**
¼ **cup date sugar**
1 **cup unsalted butter**
1 **cup chopped walnuts**
4 **ounces block carob**

    1. Butter a baking sheet lightly and set it aside.

    2. In a deep saucepan, heat the honey until it reaches 270 degrees on a candy thermometer. Remove from the heat and add the date sugar, butter, and ½ cup nuts. Mix well. Spread the candy to a thickness of ¼ inch on the prepared baking sheet. Cool.

    3. Melt the carob in the top of a double boiler over hot, not boiling, water. Cool the carob and spread it over the candy on the baking sheet. Sprinkle the remaining nuts over the carob layer. Chill the candy until hard, then break into bits or pieces.

Makes about 4 dozen pieces.

Alfalfa Fudge

½ cup honey
½ cup peanut butter
½ teaspoon pure vanilla extract
   Pinch of grated citrus peel
¾ cup chopped alfalfa sprouts
1 cup dry milk powder
¼ cup unsweetened carob powder

1. Put the honey in a saucepan and bring it to a boil. Boil for 3 minutes.

2. Pour the hot honey over the peanut butter and mix until smooth. Add the vanilla, citrus peel, and sprouts. Mix well. Use your fingers to mix in a little of the dry milk powder and carob powder. Then knead in the remaining dry milk powder and carob powder.

3. Press the candy into a greased 9-inch square pan. Chill and then cut into squares.

Makes 36 pieces.

Variations:

1. Instead of the dry milk powder, add ½ cup dry milk powder and ½ cup unsweetened carob powder.

2. Substitute another nut butter for part or all of the peanut butter.

3. Flaked coconut, wheat germ, crushed nuts, seeds, or herbs, or grated carrots may be pressed on top of the candy before it is chilled.

60-Minute Fudge

A solid, delicious and nutritious fudge.

1 pound solid carob or carob chips
1 pound sunflower seed butter
2 tablespoons honey
2 teaspoons pure black walnut or almond extract
1 cup chopped nuts

Put the carob in a heavy saucepan and melt it over very low heat. Add the sunflower seed butter and stir well. Stir in the honey, black walnut extract, and nuts. Pour the candy into a buttered 9- x 13-inch pan. Chill for 1 hour.

Makes 48 pieces.

Variation: Peanut, almond, sesame, or any other nut butter may be substituted for the sunflower seed butter.

Tootsie-Frootsie Rolls

This is a good after-school or lunch-box nibble.

½ **pound pitted dates**
   Hot water or heated herb tea
1 **ripe banana, or 1 very ripe persimmon, or**
   ½ **ripe mango**
   Unsweetened carob powder

   1. Soak the pitted dates in hot water to cover. When they are soft, add the banana and blend well. Gradually add enough carob powder to make a thick dough.

   2. Break off pieces of the dough and form them into ½- x 3-inch tootsie-sized rolls. Chill.

   Makes 24.

   Variation: The rolls may be sprinkled or dusted with something from The Spice Capsule (see page 22) before chilling.

Cherry Berries

6 **ounces roasted almond butter or cashew butter**

2 **tablespoons natural cherry concentrate**
   Sesame seeds or coconut snow (see page 23)

4 **ounces block carob, grated**

1. Mix the nut butter and cherry concentrate together. Break off pieces of the mixture and form into small balls.

2. Roll the balls in the sesame seeds to coat them.

3. Heat the grated carob in the top of a double boiler over hot, not boiling, water until it is partly melted. Remove from the heat and stir until smooth.

4. Toss 6 balls at a time in the carob sauce, lifting each out with a fork. (Catch the drippings with a spoon held in your other hand.)

5. Put the candies on wax paper and let them dry at room temperature.

Makes 24 pieces.

Variation: Any natural fruit concentrate may be substituted for the cherry concentrate.

Peanut Butter Cups

The small fluted candy cups for these little tidbits can be purchased at your local gourmet shop.

½ **cup peanut butter**
½ **cup honey or sweetened carob syrup**
½ **teaspoon pure vanilla or almond extract**
1½ **cups dry milk powder or whey powder**

1. Mix the peanut butter and honey until creamy and smooth. Stir in the vanilla. Gradually add the milk powder, mixing it in first with a spoon and then kneading it in with your fingers.

2. Break off small pieces of the dough and press them gently into fluted 1-inch paper candy cases. Store in the refrigerator in an airtight container.

Makes 18.

Variations:

1. Substitute ½ cup dry milk powder and ½ cup unsweetened carob powder for the dry milk powder.

2. Substitute sesame butter or other nut butters for all or part of the peanut butter.

3. Add small amounts of unsweetened flaked coconut, wheat germ, or ground nuts along with the dry milk powder.

Cashew Chews

½ **cup maple syrup or honey**
⅓ **cup carob chips or shredded block carob**
1 **cup raw cashews, crushed to small pieces**
1 **cup plain puffed cereal or seasoned popped popcorn**

1. Put the maple syrup in a saucepan and bring it to a boil. Remove from the heat and quickly stir in the remaining ingredients. Blend well.

2. Press the mixture into a buttered 8-inch square pan. Chill well. Cut into 24 squares or bars.

Makes 2 dozen pieces.

Born Again Granola

This cold carob and corn cereal beats the packaged variety any day.

1 **teaspoon unsalted butter**
1 **teaspoon unrefined vegetable oil**
4 **cups fresh popped unsalted popcorn**
½ **cup carob grits (see *Note*)**

   1. Preheat the oven to 300 degrees.

   2. Melt the butter and combine it with the oil. Toss the mixture with the popped corn.

   3. Spread the corn out on a baking sheet and bake until light brown. Mix in the carob grits. Serve the cereal topped with cream, milk, or carob milk.

   Makes 4 servings.

   Note: If you do not have any grits, a mixture of carob powder and ground cinnamon may be sprinkled on lightly.

Born Again Granola with Honey

½ **cup honey**
4 **cups fresh popped unsalted popcorn**
½ **cup carob grits (see *Note*)**

  1. Bring the honey to boil in a small saucepan and boil for 2 minutes.

  2. Put the popcorn in a large bowl and add the grits. Pour the warm honey over the popcorn and grits and mix well.

  3. Spread the "frosted" corn out on a greased baking sheet to cool and dry. Store in an airtight container.

  Makes 4 servings.

  Note: If you do not have any grits, a mixture of carob powder and ground cinnamon may be sprinkled on lightly.

"Cocoa" Crunch

6 ounces carob chips
½ cup unsalted butter, or ¼ cup vegetable oil
   and ¼ cup unsalted butter
1½ cups raw jumbo peanuts, cashews, almonds, or Brazil nuts, or a combination of
   these

1. Combine the carob and butter in the top of a double boiler over barely simmering water. Heat, stirring constantly, until blended to the consistency of fudge.

2. Dip the nuts, one at a time, into the hot candy. Arrange the coated nuts on a lightly buttered platter and chill until dry to the touch.

Makes 48.

Nuts Mole

Serve this snack at your next party and watch it disappear.

1 cup corn oil or corn germ oil
1 tablespoon chili powder
½ teaspoon ground cumin
   Pinch of ground coriander
2 tablespoons sifted carob powder or carob
   meal
3 cups mixed raw nuts

1. Heat the oil over low heat in a heavy skillet. Stir in the chili powder, cumin, coriander, and carob powder.

2. Mix in the nuts and stir to coat well. Turn the flame as low as possible and skillet-toast for about 10 minutes, stirring often. (You may also spread the mixture on a baking sheet and toast in a 275-degree oven, stirring frequently.)

Makes 3 cups.

Carob Jerky

This is a great snack for the hiker, biker, or backpacker. It keeps for months without refrigeration.

2 cups fresh carob pods
¼ cup thick coconut milk
¼ cup unsweetened flaked coconut

1. Seed the carob pods and put them into the container of a food processor. Process until they are ground into a coarse meal. (You may also grind the pods in a meat grinder.)

2. Combine the ground pods with the coconut milk and flaked coconut in the container of a food processor or blender. Process or blend to a very smooth purée.

3. Line a jelly-roll pan with plastic wrap, securing the edges with tape. Using a rubber spatula, spread the carob blend in the pan in an even layer. Put the pan in a gas oven with a pilot light. Let stand for 24 hours or longer, or until dry to the touch.

4. Roll up, peeling off the plastic as you roll. Leave whole, or slice into individual pieces. Wrap in plastic wrap.

Note: The jerky can also be prepared in solar ovens, dehydrators, or under a hot sun if the weather is not humid.

Figments

¾ **cup date sugar**
½ **cup prepared carob cocoa, or 1 cup carob syrup**
¼ **cup lemon juice**
1 **teaspoon grated fresh or dried orange peel**
½ **teaspoon ground cinnamon**
¼ **teaspoon ground nutmeg**
8 **ounces slit figs**

1. Combine the sugar, carob cocoa, lemon juice, orange peel, cinnamon, and nutmeg in a heavy saucepan. Cook over medium heat for about 10 minutes, stirring often. Bring to a boil, reduce the heat, and simmer for 5 minutes.

2. Put the figs in a small heat-proof bowl and pour the hot syrup over them. Cover the bowl tightly and put it on a rack to cool. When cool, refrigerate for at least 24 hours to let the flavors blend.

3. Transfer the figs to a baking pan and broil for about 3 minutes. Serve hot on toothpicks.

Makes 3 dozen pieces.

Porn

2 quarts popped popcorn
¼ cup unsalted butter or margarine
2 tablespoons carob chips
Pinch of ground cinnamon, grated orange peel, or ground mace
1 teaspoon kelp, ascorbate powder, or lecithin granules (optional)

1. Spread the popcorn out in a large baking pan.

2. Preheat the oven to 300 degrees.

3. Put the butter and carob chips in a small saucepan and melt over very low heat, stirring occasionally. Add the cinnamon and kelp and mix in well.

4. Pour the hot butter mixture over the popcorn and toss to coat the popcorn evenly. Bake 10 minutes.

Makes 2 quarts.

Carob Popcorn Balls

6 **cups popped popcorn**

1 **cup sweetened carob syrup, or ½ cup honey mixed with ½ cup unsweetened carob syrup**

1 **teaspoon white vinegar**

1 **tablespoon wheat germ**

1 **tablespoon chopped raw nuts**

1. Put the popcorn in a large mixing bowl.

2. Put the carob syrup and vinegar in a heavy saucepan and bring to a boil. Boil until it spins a thread (270 degrees or the hard-ball stage on a candy thermometer). Pour the hot syrup over popcorn immediately. Quickly mix in the wheat germ and chopped nuts.

3. When the mixture is cool enough to handle (which will be very soon), squeeze it into balls, first dipping your hands into cold water.

Makes 12 popcorn balls.

Note: You will have to work very fast to form the balls before the syrup hardens.

Beverages

Milk-Free Cocoa I

Mix equal parts of carob powder and soy milk powder. Add boiling water and blend until smooth. Sweeten with honey and flavor with vanilla. Also good cold.

Milk-Free Cocoa II

To 1 cup of hot water add 1 to 2 teaspoons any homemade carob syrup. Stir until dissolved. Add a pinch of freshly ground nutmeg and/or a dash of vanilla.

Milk-Free Mocha Cocoa I

Mix carob powder with equal parts of any herbal coffee powder. Add boiling water and sweeten to taste.

Milk-Free Mocha Cocoa II

Mix 1 teaspoon carob syrup and 1 teaspoon blackstrap molasses together. Add boiling water and stir well. A piece of cinnamon stick makes a great-tasting swizzle stick.

Café Olé

1½ quarts water
 ½ cup firmly packed date or homemade sugar
 1 cinnamon stick
 6 whole cloves
 ½ cup finely ground decaffeinated or herbal coffee powder
 2 tablespoons unsweetened carob powder

1. Combine the water, sugar, cinnamon stick, and cloves in a saucepan. Heat the mixture, stirring, for 5 minutes.

2. Stir in the ground coffee powder and carob powder. Bring to a boil, lower the heat, and simmer for 1 minute. Stir the mixture, remove from the heat, and let stand, covered, for 5 minutes. Strain into 6 coffee cups.

Makes 6 servings.

Variation: Substitute 2 cups Desweetened Carob Syrup (page 32), diluted with 2 cups water for the 1½ quarts water, and eliminate the decaffeinated or herbal coffee powder.

Iced Apricot "Coffee"

¾ cup ice-cold strong carob cocoa
½ cup carob ice cream
¼ cup apricot concentrate
Fresh mint sprig or fresh herbs for garnish

Combine all the ingredients in the container of a blender and blend until thick and foamy. Pour into a chilled 10-ounce glass.

Makes 1 serving.

Carob Coffee à la Russe

1 ounce carob chips
1½ tablespoons honey
¾ cup boiling water
1¾ cups hot strong herbal coffee or comfrey tea
½ cup scalded heavy cream
½ cup scalded milk
1 teaspoon pure vanilla extract
Ground cinnamon for garnish

1. Put the carob chips, honey, and boiling water in the top of a double boiler over hot, not boiling, water. Simmer for 3 minutes, stirring.

2. Stir in the herbal coffee, heavy cream, milk, and vanilla and mix well. Pour into 4 heated mugs and sprinkle each serving with a little cinnamon.

Makes 4 servings.

Vanilla Bean Cocoa

½ recipe for non-alcoholic vanilla (page 21)
4 tablespoons unsweetened carob powder
2 to 3 tablespoons honey
   Pinch of ground nutmeg
3 cups fresh milk
1 tablespoon lecithin granules (optional)

1. Put the vanilla extract, carob powder, honey, nutmeg, milk, and lecithin in a saucepan. Mix well.

2. Heat, stirring, but do not boil.

Makes 3 to 4 servings.

Dutch Treat

½ tablespoon honey
1 teaspoon unsulphured molasses
½ cup unsweetened carob syrup
1 cup dry milk powder
1 tablespoon pure vanilla extract
1 teaspoon brewer's yeast*
1 teaspoon lecithin granules
1½ cups water

1. Combine all the ingredients in the container of a blender and purée until smooth.

2. Pour the mixture into a heavy saucepan and heat gently, stirring constantly.

Makes 3 servings.

*To improve and mellow the flavor of the yeast, mix all the ingredients together and refrigerate overnight.

Mock Chocolate Milk

1. Soak sunflower seeds for 24 hours in leftover carob cocoa or milk.

2. Put the seeds and cocoa mix in the container of a blender and blend with just enough additional water or milk to give the desired texture and frothiness.

Variations: For lots of froth, add 1 or 2 ice cubes to the mixture while blending. For a thicker mixture, add 1 or 2 teaspoons milk or whey powder to the mixture before you blend it.

Crunchy "Chocolate" Milk

½ **cup cold milk**
1 **ripe banana, peeled and cut into chunks**
1 **to 2 pitted dates, chopped**
1 **to 2 teaspoons unsweetened carob powder**
1 **or more teaspoons coarsely crushed sunflower seeds**

Put all the ingredients, with the exception of the sunflower seeds, in the container of a blender and blend until smooth and creamy. Stir in the sunflower seeds just before serving.

Makes 1 serving.

Low-Calorie Liquid Brownies

¾ cup hot water
2 tablespoons rose hips powder*
2 tablespoons unsweetened carob powder
2 tablespoons dry milk powder
3 cups hot scalded skim milk

Combine all the ingredients, with the exception of the hot skim milk, in the container of a blender. Blend at high speed until smooth. Turn the blender to low speed and add the hot skim milk slowly. Serve immediately.

Makes 3 servings.

*Rose hips powder is available in health food stores. If you cannot find it you can use pulverized whole dried rose hips.

Devil Shake

1½ cups carob cocoa
2 tablespoons carob syrup
1 tablespoon instant herbal coffee powder
1 cup sparkling mineral water

Combine the carob cocoa, carob syrup, and coffee powder in the container of blender or in a large cocktail shaker. Blend or shake until the mixture is foamy. Pour in the mineral water and serve.

Makes 2 servings.

5
Carob in Healing

A cup of carob cocoa to cure your diarrhea? A piece of carob fudge to remedy constipation? A carob candy bar to raise your depleted mineral reserves? Yes, indeed, carob is one of Mother Nature's nicer non-toxic crutches.

In a study of 230 infants with diarrhea (reported in the June 1953 issue of the _Canadian Medical Association Journal_), only three were not cured by the addition of carob powder to their formula. The treatment apparently worked because carob contains high levels of fiber, pectin, and lignin, concluded the study, which recent research shows can clear up digestive problems, including vomiting and diarrhea.

"Pectin," reports one researcher, "is effective in combining with certain harmful elements of radioactive fallout and carrying them harmlessly out of the body.... European doctors have used carob flour extensively, believing that both the pectin and the lignin it contains are beneficial...."

Carob is a natural pick-me-up because it is naturally sweet. So when you have depleted your energy supply through exercise, munch on a carob bar to correct the sodium/potassium balance in your body. Unlike chocolate, carob is alkaline and readily assimilated.

Here are some remedial ways to use carob.

Ex-Flax

Flax is one of the more famous of nature's laxatives (used in moderation), while whey is a well-known digestive aid. They combine well with carob with its high bulk-forming fiber and pectin.

4   tablespoons flaxseed meal
1   tablespoon unsweetened carob syrup
1   tablespoon powdered whey (optional)
4   figs, soaked, drained, and minced
    Dash of pure vanilla extract or oil of peppermint

1. Put all the ingredients in the container of a blender and purée until smooth.

2. Roll into small balls and chill. You can also press the mixture into a small sesame seed-coated pan, chill, and cut it into small squares.

Little Dippers

This is an excellent anti-diarrhea aid.

12   large whole, peak-of-the-season strawberries or fresh flower blossoms
4   ounces block carob
1   tablespoon toasted flaxseed
1   tablespoon raw carob or whey powder

1. Wash and dry the fruit very well.

2. Break the carob into fairly uniform chunks and put the chunks into the top of a double boiler.

Melt the carob over hot, not boiling, water. Stir until smooth.

3. Grasp each berry by the hull and swirl it in the melted carob, allowing the carob to cover about two thirds of the fruit. Carefully put the coated berry on wax paper and sprinkle it with the flaxseed and powder. Repeat the process with the remaining berries. (If the carob begins to harden before you are finished coating the berries, reheat it over hot water.)

4. Keep the berries on the wax paper until the coating hardens. (You can refrigerate the berries to speed the process, if you want.) Transfer to a serving plate.

Note: For a touch of luxury, rinse the berries in white wine, champagne, sparkling grape juice, or sparkling mineral water before dipping.

Mr. Softee

This is a good stool softener. Take two or three cups daily.

2 hard-boiled eggs
⅓ cup soft chopped dates, prunes, figs, or apricots
2 tablespoons unsweetened carob powder
1 teaspoon pure vanilla extract
½ cup unrefined vegetable oil

1. Combine the eggs and dates in the container of a blender.

2. Slowly add the remaining ingredients and purée until smooth. Spoon into small cups and chill or freeze.

Enerjets

¾ **cup honey**
⅓ **cup water**
¼ **teaspoon cream of tartar**
1 **pound pitted prunes**

   1. Combine the honey and water in a sauce-pan and boil until the mixture is amber colored. (Do not stir during the boiling.) Stir the cream of tartar into the mixture just before you take it from the stove.

   2. Spread the prunes out on a buttered baking sheet and pour the syrup over them. Let sit until hardened. Store in the refrigerator in an airtight container.

   Note: You can sprinkle the coated prunes with any of the dusting powders on page 23.

Electrolyte Replacement Powder

When exercise has depleted your energy supply, try drinking some of this.

½ **cup unsweetened carob powder**
3 **tablespoons brewer's yeast**
¼ **cup dry milk powder or whey powder**
1 **teaspoon kelp and/or ascorbate powder**
   Ground seeds or nuts, honey, or pure vanilla extract to taste (optional)
4 **cups skim milk**

   1. Mix the carob powder, yeast, dry milk powder, and kelp together. Store in the refrigerator in a screw-top jar.

2. When ready to serve, combine with the milk in the container of a blender.

Makes 4 to 6 servings.

High-fiber carob even helps to fight fat. Rich in natural carbohydrates, carob is 40 percent natural sugar. It may not be a cure-all for your sweet tooth, but it is a big help. Try this safe and sane 50-calorie-a-square appetite suppressant.

Diet-Bites

1 cup maple syrup
1 cup unsweetened carob syrup
4 tablespoons unsalted butter
1 tablespoon lecithin granules

1. Put the maple syrup, carob syrup, and butter into a large heavy saucepan. Bring to a boil and boil until the mixture registers 234 degrees on a candy thermometer, or until it just holds together when dropped into cold (not iced) water. Remove from the heat and let cool to lukewarm.

2. When the mixture is lukewarm, beat the mixture until it begins to lose its gloss. Stir in the lecithin granules. Pour the mixture into a lightly buttered 8- x 4-inch loaf pan and cut it into 50 small squares before it has hardened.

Makes 50 pieces.

Old-Fashioned Vinegar and Horehound Cough Drops

Try these when that common cold gets you down.

2 **ounces dried horehound**
   Hot water
2 **cups carob syrup**
½ **cup unpasteurized apple cider vinegar**
½ **cup water**
1 **teaspoon unsalted butter**
½ **teaspoon baking soda, dissolved in water**

   1. Cover the horehound with hot water and soak overnight.

   2. Put the soaked horehound, carob syrup, vinegar, and ½ cup water into a saucepan. Heat quickly to 240 degrees on a candy thermometer. Add the butter and continue to cook until the mixture registers 270 degrees on the thermometer. Stir in the dissolved baking soda just before removing the pan from the heat.

   3. When the candy is cool enough to handle, pull by hand (like taffy) and use scissors to snip it into drops. Let dry at room temperature. Store in an airtight container.

   If you have cosmetic allergies, try this face powder instead of a commercial brand:

Carob Face Powder

½ **cup soybean powder**
   Carob powder

   Combine the soybean powder in a plastic bag with enough carob powder to get the desired color. Knead together well. Sift to remove any coarse particles.

   Carob pods are also good for the family's dog. Break the whole pods in half, seed them, and let the pet chew away at the broken pods. Or, try baking up this snack for the dog:

Boners

   1 **package active dry yeast**
   ¼ **cup warm water**
   1 **cup broth**
2½ **cups whole wheat flour**
   ½ **cup cornmeal**
   1 **cup cracked wheat**
   ½ **cup unsweetened carob powder**
   1 **egg, beaten**

   1. Sprinkle the yeast over the warm water and let it soften. Then mix it well with the broth.
   2. Measure the flour, cornmeal, cracked wheat, and carob powder into a large bowl. Pour in the liquid and mix well. Add more broth if the dough is too stiff.
   3. Preheat the oven to 300 degrees.

4. Roll the dough out to a thickness of ¼ inch on a floured board. Cut into bones. Put the bones on a lightly buttered baking sheet.

5. Brush each bone with the beaten egg and bake for 45 minutes. Leave in the oven overnight to dry.

Makes about 50 2-inch biscuits.

Appendices

CAROB POWDER vs. COCOA POWDER
Typical Composition and Nutritional Data

	Carob Powder	Cocoa Non-Alkali Processed
Calories per 100 grams (approx. 3½ oz.)	380	410
Protein	3.8 %	23.0%
Total Carbohydrates (as sugars and fiber)	90.6 %	56.5%
Sugars (as invert) (3)	45.5 %	2.0%
Crude Fiber (3)	5.4 %	8.5%
Fat	0.2 %	10.0%
Moisture	2.6 %	2.5%
Ash (mineral matter)	2.8 %	5.5%
Calcium (mg./100 g.)	290	600
Iron (mg./100 g.)	2	10
Sodium (mg./100 g.)	10	10
Potassium (mg./100 g.)	800	1,500
Caffeine (mg./100 g.)	none detected	180
Theobromine (mg./100 g.)	3	2,320

The calorie values listed above have been calculated using values of 9 calories per gram of fat and 4 calories per gram of carbohydrate or protein. These values do *not* take into consideration the fact that a portion of the carbohydrates, generally dietary fiber, may be calorically nonavailable. Literature values for the calorie content of carob flour indicate approximately 200 calories per 100 grams (USDA Handbook #8) and for cocoa powder (medium fat) about 290 calories per 100 grams (cocoa manufacturer's data).

CAROB COCOA vs. HOT CHOCOLATE

	Made with whole milk (per cup)	Made with whole milk (per cup)
Protein	8.74 g.	8.21 g.
Fat	9.7 g.	12.5 g.
Carbohydrates	20.8 g.	26.2 g.
Calories	204	239

Source: USDA Handbook #8.

Measure for Measure

The following is a list of combinations of ingredients, such as liquid to flour in batters, that you can use as a reference when you are cooking or baking. It should really be called "Why It Works," because it does explain the proportions of ingredients in recipes.

1 cup liquid to 1 cup flour for pour batters
1 cup liquid to 2 cups flour for drop batters
1 cup liquid to 3 cups flour for dough
⅓ to 2 or more cakes of compressed yeast softened

in ½ cup water to 2 cups liquid (⅓ yeast cake to 2 cups liquid is used in bread mixed at night; 1 cake or more can be added to bread mixed in the morning, according to the time available for rising. By using several yeast cakes to 2 cups liquid, bread may be baked in 3 or 4 hours from the time of mixing.)

½ cup liquid yeast to 2 cups liquid

1 teaspoon baking soda and 3½ level teaspoons cream of tartar to 4 cups flour

2 teaspoons baking powder to 1 cup flour, when eggs are not used

1 teaspoon baking soda to 2 cups thick sour milk

1 teaspoon baking soda to 1 cup molasses

¼ teaspoon salt to 4 cups milk for custards

¼ teaspoon salt to 1 cup, or 1 teaspoon to 4 cups of sauce or soup

1 teaspoon flavoring extract to 4 cups of custard or cream

1 tablespoon flavoring extract to 4 cups mixture to be frozen

⅔ cup (or less) sugar to 4 cups milk for custards

1 cup sugar to 4 cups milk or cream for ice cream

4 eggs to 4 cups milk for plain custard

6 to 8 eggs to 4 cups milk for molded custards

¼ package (or ½ ounce) gelatin to 2 cups (scant) liquid

Nutritional Composition of Other Flours vs. Carob Flour

Food and Description (dry)	Calories (per 100 g.)	Protein (g.)	Fat (g.)	Fiber (g.)	Carbo-hydrates (g.)	Minerals (per 100 g.)		Vitamins (per 100 g.)	
Carob Flour 1 tsp. = 2 g.	351	7.75	1.9	5.05	72.85	210 mg. calcium	50. I.U.A.	.033 mg. B_1	
						120 mg. phosphorus		.053 mg. B_2	
						5 mg. iron		2.53 mg. niacin	
						950 mg. potassium			
						80 mg. magnesium			
						10 mg. silicon			
Unbleached White Flour (hard wheat) 1 cup = 112 g.	365	11.8	1.1	.3	74.4	16 mg. calcium		.08 mg. B_1	
						95 mg. phosphorus		.06 mg. B_2	
						.9 mg. iron		1.00 mg. niacin	
Buckwheat Flour	347	11.7	2.5	1.6	70.4	33 mg. calcium		.58 mg. B_1	
						347 mg. phosphorus		.15 mg. B_2	
						2.8 mg. iron		2.99 mg. niacin	

About the Author

FRANCES SHERIDAN GOULART is the forty-five-year-old Detroit-born author of *How to Write a Cookbook and Sell It* (Ashley Books: 1980), *Eating to Win: Food Psyching for the Athlete* (Stein & Day: 1978), *Bum Steers: How to Make Your Own Meat Substitutes* (Chatham Press: 1975), *Bone Appetit: Natural Petfood Recipes* (Pacific Search: 1976), *The Mother Goose Cookbook* (Price, Stern, Sloan: 1970).

In 1981 Guide Books published her "mini" books *501 Household Hints, All About Cats,* and *The Book of Remedies: Advice for Athletes.* Also in 1981 Alfred Publishing Company published *Vegetarian Cooking Made Easy.* This year Simon & Schuster published her trade paperback *The Vegetarian Weight Loss Cookbook.* Coming in 1983, Everest House will publish Ms. Goulart's *Nutritional Self-Defense: Protecting Yourself from Yourself,* Stein & Day will publish *The Eating to Win Cookbook,* and Simon & Schuster will publish her *True Confections: 101 Non-Allergenic Desserts.*

Ms. Goulart is the founder-director of The Potsanjammer School of Natural Cooking in Fairfield County, Connecticut.

She is a regular contributor to dozens of magazines and journals including *Runner's World, American Bee Journal, Body Builders, Muscle Up, Surfing, Muscle Digest, Boy's Life, Running and Fitness, New Body, Shape, Beauty Digest,* and *Vegetarian Times.*

In her spare hours Ms. Goulart is a competitive long-distance runner, a squash and racquetball player, and one of Connecticut's top female runners, with many titles and trophies to her credit.

Ms. Goulart is an active member of the AAU, the American Medical Writers Association, the Natural Foods Association, Nutrition Today Society, the National Health Federation, the International Women's Writing Guild, the International Academy of Nutritional Consultants, and the Human Ecology Action League. She is listed in Who's Who (American Authors Edition), as well as Michigan's Who's Who. Ms. Goulart is a researcher and also lectures frequently.

In private life she is the wife of science fiction writer Ron Goulart. They live in Weston, Connecticut, with their two sons.

LOOK AND FEEL BETTER WITH THESE WARNER BOOKS

HOW TO LOOK TEN YEARS YOUNGER
by Adrien Arpel (L97-823, $8.95)
Adrien Arpel, president of her own multi-million dollar company, tells you how to give yourself a 10-years-younger image in just one day via her 5-step repackaging system; how to lift and trim your body in 10 minutes a day; how to follow the 24-hour emergency diet. She will also show you how to dress to hide body flaws as well as how to use make-up and win the big six skin battles to be wrinkle-free.

Large format paperback

THE 15-MINUTE-A-DAY NATURAL FACELIFT
by M. J. Saffron *L37-325, $4.95 U.S.A./L37-326, $5.95 Canada*
Now you can give yourself all the beautifying effects of a face lift—safely and naturally without surgery—through a unique series of exercises created by international beauty expert M. J. Saffron. And it will take just minutes a day!

Large format paperback

YOUTHLIFT
by M. J. Saffron *L97-816, $4.95 U.S.A./L37-274, $5.95 Canada*
Prevent the signs of age, banish them if they've begun, erase them and look young again. In your own home you can exercise away wrinkles, sags, and grooves from the areas where age shows first—neck, chin, and shoulders.

KEEP YOURSELF HEALTHY!

Available in paperback

Earl Mindell's VITAMIN BIBLE   *(L93613-8 $2.95)*

tells you all about vitamins and what they can do for you.
- How vitamin needs vary for each of us, and how to determine your own needs.

- How to determine if you need supplements and how to pick the right one.

- What the current Recommended Daily Allowances of all vitamins and nutrients are.

- How to substitute natural substances for tranquilizers and drugs.

- How vitamins can improve sex, combat a desire for alcohol, lower cholesterol levels, fight depression, help your heart.

- Vitamin precautions everyone should know.

- Which vitamins work together for the most potent effect.

- Plus...listing of the vitamin and nutrient content of hundreds of common foods.

SUGAR BLUES
by William Dufty   *(30-512, $3.95)*

Like opium, morphine, and heroin, sugar is an addictive drug, yet Americans consume it daily in everything from cigarettes to bread. If you are overweight, or suffer from migraine, hypoglycemia or acne, the plague of the Sugar Blues has hit you. In fact, by accepted diagnostic standards, *our entire society is pre-diabetic*. *Sugar Blues* shows you how to live better without it and includes recipes for delicious dishes —all sugar-free!

HEALTHY EATING
FROM WARNER BOOKS

Available in large-format quality paperback

THE ALLERGY COOKBOOK & FOOD-BUYING GUIDE
by Pamela P. Nonken and S. Roger Hirsch, M.D.   *(L37173, $6.95)*

Are you allergic to corn, eggs, milk, soy, wheat, or yeast?

This important guide:

- Lists what foods are safe to buy...both by category and by brand name.
- Lists foods to avoid—where allergens may be ingredients though unlabeled.
- Identifies allergens in all their names and forms.
- Offers hints and foods to substitute for allergens in adapting your recipes.
- Contains a recipe book that eliminates specific allergens—300 delicious dishes all cross-referenced for quick and easy use.

Available in hardcover

DC SUPER HEROES SUPER HEALTHY COOKBOOK
by Mark Saltzman, Judy Garlan & Michele Grodner with a foreword by Dr. Joan Gussow   *(L51227-3, $8.95)*

Good food kids can make themselves!

Your kids will have loads of fun with their favorite comic book characters while learning how to put together nutritious meals including:

Plastic Man's Spaghetti & Meatballs

Hawkman's Egg Birds

Krypton Krunch Cereal

Wonder Woman's Natural Soda Pop

Superman's Super Delicious Still Nutritious Party Cake and much much more.

ESPECIALLY FOR YOU

IMPROVE YOUR HEALTH
WITH WARNER BOOKS

LOW SALT SECRETS FOR YOUR DIET
by Dr. William J. Vaughan   *(L37-223, $3.95)*
Not just for people who must restrict salt intake, but for everyone!
Forty to sixty million Americans have high blood pressure, and nearly
one million Americans die of heart disease every year. Hypertension,
often called the silent killer, can be controlled by restricting your
intake of salt. This handy pocket-size guide can tell you how much salt
is hidden in more than 2,600 brand-name and natural foods.

THE CORNER DRUGSTORE   *large format paperback:*
by Max Leber   *(L97-989, $6.95 U.S.A./L37-278, $8.50 Canada)*
In simple, down-to-earth language, THE CORNER DRUGSTORE
(Coming in January) provides complete coverage of the over-the-
counter products and services available at your local pharmacy. Here's
everything you should know about everything that pharmacies sell, a
working knowledge that will save you money and enable you to use
nonprescription drugs and health aids more wisely.

Look for this—and other Warner bestsellers—in your bookstore. If
you can't find them, you may order directly from us by sending
your check or money order for the retail price of the book, plus 50¢
per order and 50¢ per copy to cover postage and handling, to:
WARNER BOOKS, P.O. Box 690, New York, NY 10019. New
York State and California residents must add applicable sales tax.
Please allow 4 weeks for delivery of your books.